KANPUR TO KOLKATA

Labour Recruitment for the Sugar Colonies

EDITED AND INTRODUCED BY
BASDEO MANGRU

H
HANSIB

First published in 2015
by Hansib Publications Limited

P.O. Box 226, Hertford, Hertfordshire
SG14 3WY, United Kingdom
info@hansibpublications.com

www.hansibpublications.com

Copyright © Dr Basdeo Mangru, 2014

ISBN 978-1-910553-00-8

All rights reserved.
Without limiting the rights under copyright reserved above,
no part of this publication may be reproduced, stored in or
introduced into a retrieval system, or transmitted, in any form
or by any means (electronic, mechanical, photocopying,
recording or otherwise), without the prior written permission
of both the copyright owner and the publisher of this book.

A CIP catalogue record for this book
is available from the British Library

Production by Hansib Publications Limited
Printed in Great Britain

For Brandon Ajay, Jaya Sonali and Ray Anthony

ACKNOWLEDGEMENTS

In preparing this volume for publication, the Editor has received guidance and support from several sources. I would like to thank the British Library, the original source of this Report, for granting Copyright Permission to publish it from its official collections. I am most grateful to Leela Ramotar, Educator, for her sustained efforts in locating this unpublished, uncatalogued document in the India Office Records at the British Library in London. Her patience, diligence and determination have been remarkable. I acknowledge my heartfelt thanks also to Dr Gary Girdhari, former Senior Lecturer and Head of the Biology Department, University of Guyana, for his meticulous review of the text and his invaluable editorial advice and constructive criticism. The unstinted support of Jack Mangra, Netram Rambudhan, Vince Ramcharran and members of the Association of Artists and Writers is gratefully appreciated. My colleagues in the Department of History and Philosophy at York College, City University of New York, have been most supportive. Throughout my academic career Dr Mary Noel-Menezes, Professor Emeritus, University of Guyana, has been a pillar of support and a constant source of inspiration, particularly through her meticulous, sustained scholarship. Finally, I wish to record my gratitude to Doreen, Ray and Tricia for their enthusiastic support and invaluable comments, and for clerical and technical assistance in finalizing the manuscript for publication.

Whatever may be the result of my tour, I at least shall retain a strong feeling of satisfaction at the recollection of the evident gratitude of many of these poor people to hear from me that relatives whom they had long given up as dead might yet be alive and well, and might possibly either return or be communicated with.

D.G. Pitcher, Diary

CONTENTS

Map of India
5

*Civil Divisions and Districts of the
North-Western Provinces and Oudh*
6

Acknowledgements
7

Preface
9

Introduction
11

*Report on the System of Recruiting
Labourers for the Colonies, 1882*
21

Appendices
64

*Diary of tour in the North-Western Provinces and
Oudh while on Special Duty in connection with
emigration to the Colonies from British India*
80

Glossary
154

Further Reading
160

About the Editor
162

Index
163

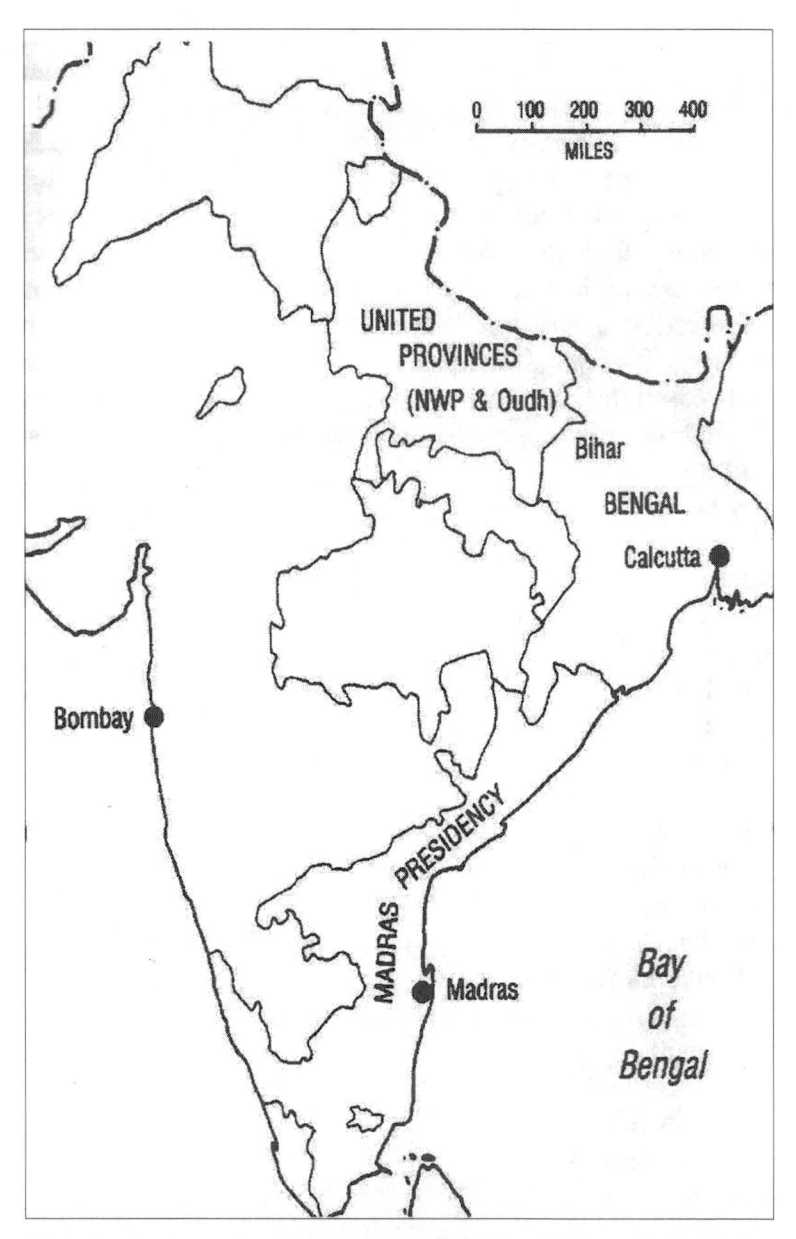

Map showing contemporary Uttar Pradesh (U.P.) and other recruiting areas

Civil Divisions and Districts of the North-Western Provinces and Oudh

Agra Division
Agra
Etah
Etawah
Farukhabad
Muttra
Mainpuri

Allahabad Division
Allahabad
Banda
Kanpur
Fatehpur
Hamirpur
Jaunpur

Benares Division
Azamgarh
Ballia
Basti
Benares
Ghazipur
Gorakhpur
Mirzapur

Meerut Division

Rohilkhan Division

Fyzabad Division
Bahraich
Fyzabad
Gonda

Lucknow Division
Bara Banki
Lucknow
Unao

Rai Bareli Division
Partabgarh
Rae Bareli
Sultanpur

PREFACE

Kanpur to Kolkata (historically Cawnpore to Calcutta, the terms used throughout this volume) is essentially a reproduction of aspects of the unpublished Report *cum* Diary of Major D. G. Pitcher, a Judge in the Indian Civil Service. He was commissioned in late 1882 to undertake a comprehensive study of colonial recruiting operations in the North-Western Provinces and Oudh, an administrative district under a Lieutenant-Governor, which existed between 1856 and 1902, and as the United Provinces between 1902 and 1947. Today this vast region is the State of Uttar Pradesh, the fifth largest in the Indian Union with a population of roughly 190 million and a capital city, Lucknow.

Besides Hugh Tinker, the pioneering historian in the field, very few scholars/researchers, including those in the academic community, have utilized or mentioned this primary source in their published works. This is somewhat surprising as its wealth of information and key statistical data make such an eyewitness account indispensable. Perhaps scholars are unaware of its existence for it is not even catalogued in the emigration proceedings of the Government of India housed in the India Office Collections at the British Library in London. Its publication may perhaps open up new vistas in this fascinating field.

This study is valuable in several respects. It provides new insights into emigration issues which are hardly mentioned in the literature. That the sub-agency business was "to a strident extent" monopolized by Jews, who first arrived in India over two thousand years ago and evolved as three different communities, is certainly revealing. It highlights also the fact that many villagers disposed to emigrate came from even Native States not under the British Raj and from different socio-economic backgrounds, and were not always the "dregs" of Indian society. It provides, for example, evidence of emigrants displaying an entrepreneurial spirit, investing small fortunes in such luxury items as *tika* for women, *attar* and scents to resell to Indians resident in the colonies. It details up-country depot operations and physical conditions, the various obstacles to emigration provided by government officials, *zamindars, banias* and others, rail transportation facilities (a distance of roughly 685 miles from Cawnpore to Calcutta), and exposes the intimidatory and extortionary practices of rural policemen. The disclosure that prostitution was prevalent in the depots and that women recruiters were employed in the service, albeit on a limited scale, throw fresh light on the recruiting process as such information is conspicuously absent in the published sources. Pitcher's interviews with returned emigrants provide nuggets of information indispensable to the researcher.

Even more significant are the insights into the grief and trauma in rural India emanating from the departure of friends, families and loved ones for unknown lands. This largely neglected field of enquiry is only now engaging scholarly attention since for decades the focus on Indian diasporic research largely concentrated on their transplantation and experiences under the iniquitous indenture system. Accordingly, the trauma of colonial emigration in Village India had been ignored. Within recent years, scholars, particularly in Suriname where the Bhojpuri culture and tradition predominate and continue to flourish, have alluded to the pain and pathos surrounding such separation. It seemed to produce "a distinct folk culture" in the Bhojpuri-speaking regions of Bihar and Uttar Pradesh. Accordingly, the term 'Bidesia' affectionately encompasses not only those in the diaspora but also the folk culture created in their memory. Pitcher's conversations with parents and wives longing (some for nearly 18 years) to hear from departed ones, his concerns at their plight and his willingness and determination to provide relevant information through Indian authorities, will hopefully produce a spurt in research activities on the 'Bidesia'.

INTRODUCTION

Indians, who today form roughly 20 per cent of the English-speaking Caribbean, were introduced into the region as part of the sugar planters' post-emancipation efforts to tap an alternative and competitive labour supply to supplement the truculent ranks of the existing workforce. Freedom had conferred on the emancipated workers both spatial and occupational mobility which the planting interests considered anathemical to the resuscitation of the sugar industry. They saw immigration as the antidote to emancipation for it would not only enable them to divide the workforce both ethnically and culturally but also to create competition for employment and simultaneously reduce wages as well. Accustomed as they were to a mentality of coerced labour, the planting interests introduced immigrants from practically the habitable globe. India with its teeming millions in densely populated areas became the main reservoir of colonial manpower.

Throughout the nearly eighty years of organised emigration from India (1838-1917), the port of embarkation in North India was Calcutta (Kolkata) and Madras (Chennai) in South India. North Indian recruits, up to the 1860s, comprised principally tribal people from the hilly, inaccessible areas of Chota Nagpur, with a sprinkling of indigents from the Calcutta metropolitan area and the Twenty-Four Parganas and its environs. With the drying up of labour from this region, largely through high mortality at sea and heavy demand by tea planters of Assam, recruiting activities were extended north-westwards with the main concentration being the North-Western Provinces and Oudh, and the western part of the vast Bengal Presidency from which the Province of Bihar was created in 1912. Eventually western Bihar and eastern Uttar Pradesh, the Bhojpuri-speaking regions, became the catchment area which supplied the majority of emigrants. By 1882, nearly two-thirds of the recruits were enlisted in this region and one-sixth in Bengal and Bihar.[1] This pattern of labour recruitment from North India continued to increase until the demise of the system during the First World War. In the decade, 1890-1900, for example, the North-Western Provinces and Oudh exported an average of 78 per cent of colonial recruits.

In the early phase of colonial recruitment several expatriate Calcutta firms, notably Gillander, Arbuthnot and Company,[2] procured labour for colonial employers. When the export of labour became government-controlled in the 1840s, the recruitment system became more uniform. Each recipient colony appointed an Emigration Agent of approved character who established a depot at Calcutta, principally at Garden Reach. The Agents were expected to employ licensed recruiters of respectable character to enlist villagers by legitimate means and register their engagement before the *mufassal* (district) magistrate. The recruits were conveyed to Calcutta or Madras in batches and housed in licensed depots under the Agent's vigilance. Following a brief depot residence, they were shipped in licensed vessels which were expected to be well equipped, fully provisioned and sea-worthy for a three-month trans-Atlantic passage. These requirements were considered necessary to ensure health, safety and comfort in transit to the importing colonies.

In the colonies, Indian authorities expected the immigrants to be treated on a par with "the more robust races of the West."[3] They required, concomitantly, that wages and other contractual terms were "fully and clearly stated" and that employers provide "efficient protection" against tyranny and neglect, and adequate medical and legal protection as well. Additionally, the Indian Government stipulated that in relation to the distant West Indian colonies a free return passage be provided at the termination of the contract.[4]

With the lapse of time, the extension of recruiting operations over vast areas, the employment of unlicensed recruiters called *Arkatis* and lack of effective supervision of recruiters' activities, a phalanx of abuses crept up. But the basic structure of recruiting operations hardly underwent any radical change save in its administrative structure and the overwhelming need to minimise abuses and prevent untoward criticism.

RECRUITING ABUSE

By the 1850s recruiting abuses, which began with the commencement of the immigration system, had become more prevalent. The most glaring was the interception of batches of recruits and decoying them through bribes, intimidation and deception to rival agencies. Such irregularities prompted the Mauritius Government, whose Agency suffered most on account of its popularity, efficient recruiting system and thorough depot medical examination, to depute H.N.D. Beyts, Protector of Immigrants and an Eurasian fluent in Indian languages, to investigate the problem. He alleged that recruiting operations were "radically defective,"[5] and that fraud, misrepresentation and forced detention permeated the entire system.

Beyts adumbrated several key recommendations chiefly with regard to licensing and badging of recruiters, medical examination and registration of recruits, fines and punishments for irregularities and the use of sign boards painted in English and Indian languages to identify the various colonial depots. Predictably his laudable suggestions encountered stiff opposition from colonial agents anxious to minimise expenditure, remove administrative obstacles and avoid unnecessary delays.[6] They objected strenuously to recruiters appearing with recruits at the Protector's office for registration because of varying distances (from 2 to 600 miles). They opposed, furthermore, the suggestion that recruiters accompany recruits to Calcutta which they considered unnecessary, time-consuming and physically taxing.

Beyts' principal recommendations, with modifications proposed by the Government of Bengal, were incorporated in Consolidated Ordinance 4 of 1864. This was the first major piece of legislation on recruitment by Indian authorities since the suspension of emigration in 1839. The Act consolidated the emigration laws contained in sixteen acts passed from 1839 to 1860. It provided, inter alia, for the licensing and badging of the recruiter, confining him to a single Agency and requiring him to appear with his recruits before the *mufassal* magistrate for examination and registration.[7] It was now mandatory for each importing colony to establish a depot which would be inspected, approved and licensed, thus rendering private depots illegal. Additionally, for the first time the duties of the Protector of Emigrants at Calcutta were legally defined.

These elaborate provisions represented, in theory at least, a substantial improvement at reforming and regularising the recruitment process. In practice, pressure from colonial agents and socio-economic conditions in India tended to stymie the enforcement of official policies. Having received money advances which they could hardly repay and extricate themselves, prospective recruits, caught in a hopeless economic and psychological situation, had no other alternative but to emigrate. It was thus difficult to enforce legislation designed to remedy existing defects and minimise abuses.

UP-COUNTRY DEPOTS

The establishment of sub-depots in the mid-1860s, as recruitment shifted north-westwards, tended to multiply abuses. The sub-agents who manned these establishments were largely unlicensed men who were immune from prosecution as they did not fall under the purview of the 1864 Act. Not only were they appointed without reference to their character but also some were former recruiters dismissed from the service, and seemed to exercise little supervisory control over recruiters in their employ. Moreover, the system of remuneration, based on a capitation fee *cum* bonus, tended to intensify competition among recruiters, which correspondingly perpetuated abuses and irregularities. The customary but lawful use of *Arkatis* to establish initial contacts with prospective recruits produced a high incidence of entrapment and illegal detention. Indian women were particularly vulnerable to the golden blandishments of glib recruiters. The paucity of women recruits coupled with high remuneration for their procurement made them highly prized. An article entitled 'An Indian Slave Trade' in the *Pioneer of India*, an Anglo-Indian newspaper established at Allahabad, alluded in 1871 to the case of Ratunya, a young, beautiful woman, who was accosted by a recruiter, offered employment and forcibly detained. She and others were only released through the timely intervention of two missionaries.[8]

The spate of abductions, unlawful detention and deception reinforced by the charge of a revival of slavery, demanded government action. The reports of several *mufassal* magistrates relating to frequent kidnapping attempts likewise emphasised the need for reform. The result was the promulgation of new rules under Act VII of 1871, which was largely consolidatory, to bolster defective provisions of the 1864 Act.[9] Nevertheless, efforts by Indian authorities to minimise recruiting malpractices were often thwarted by pressure from Colonial Agents. The economic interests of employers thus proved a formidable obstacle to the enforcement of policies formulated in India. Indian authorities were cognisant of the economic benefits of emigration and realised that recruiting obstacles and escalating expenses might effectively check the system.

INDIAN GOVERNMENT POLICY

Persistent complaints by colonial Emigration Agents against the seemingly obstructionist attitude of *mufassal* magistrates, prompted the West India Committee, the planters' influential lobby at Whitehall, to initiate a meeting with Lord Salisbury, Secretary of State for India. At this meeting, held at the India Office in London on 25 January 1875, Neville Lubbock, the Committee's assiduous Deputy Chairman, and his associates voiced concerns at the non-encouragement of emigration by Indian authorities. The essence of the Committee's views was that the export of Indian labour overseas enhanced the socio-economic position of Indian villagers and should be promoted actively.[10]

The result was Salisbury's despatch Number 39 of 24 March 1875 which Tinker labelled the "Magna Carta of the liberties of Indians in the British colonies."[11] The despatch not only advocated active encouragement of emigration, especially during times of economic distress, but also suggested ways of implementing it. One urged the Indian Government to assume direct responsibility for the accuracy of information disseminated in the *mufassal* and for the performance of contractual terms.[12] Salisbury also requested the Government of India to consider such issues as abolishment of the return passage entitlement, reduction in emigration expenses and the educational upliftment and general benefit of emigration to Indians.[13]

The Government of India responded over two years later after consulting the relevant provincial governments. It decided against direct encouragement of emigration largely because of the probable impact on the minds of Indians. It preferred instead to maintain the existing policy of benevolent neutrality adopted since the commencement of emigration. It asserted:

> After a careful consideration of the past history of Indian emigration, and of the probable effect on the native mind of a direct intervention on the part of Government to

encourage its subjects to emigrate, we are clearly of opinion that any material departure from the permissive attitude which has hitherto been observed would be extremely impolitic.[14]

Nevertheless, Indian authorities gave assurances which considerably appeased the plantocracy. Its officials would acquaint themselves fully with wage levels and conditions of service offered by various recipient colonies so that they could communicate this information with some confidence. Furthermore, the Indian Government undertook to remove unnecessary obstacles in the recruiting process, especially with regard to a circular emanating from the Government of the North Western Provinces and Oudh instructing its officers to refuse the registration of women resident in other districts.[15]

The trend towards encouragement of emigration continued in the 1880s. It seemed to emanate from favourable reports by colonial authorities, especially in British Guiana, on the Indian Emigration Bill of 1880.[16] It was during discussion of this Bill in the recipient colonies that the Government of India advised local and provincial governments in the principal recruiting areas of northern India to conduct their own investigation into recruiting operations in the *mufassal*. Two invaluable reports resulted from these enquiries – one by Major D.G. Pitcher in the North-Western Provinces and Oudh in 1882, and the other by G.A. Grierson in 1883 in the Bengal Presidency, particularly the Bihari districts and the Twenty-Four Parganas, the industrial suburb of Calcutta.

Pitcher was deputed by the Government of India to enquire into the system of emigration from British India to certain French and British Colonies as conducted in the North-Western Provinces and Oudh. A Judge of the Small Cause Court in Lucknow, Pitcher received a fixed allowance of Rs. 200 a month including travelling expenses.[17] His terms of reference were broad and varied. He was mandated to, inter alia, provide details of depot arrangements and management, ascertain the class and character of colonial recruiters, pronounce on the state of the labour market, assess the attitude of Indian women towards emigration overseas, evaluate the registration process and determine the type of reforms needed to enhance the whole registration process. Pitcher was instructed, furthermore, to report on the key issues of family emigration and female recruitment, to ascertain the various local objections to emigration and determine why emigration was more popular in some districts than in others.

Besides providing information on vital emigration issues, Pitcher was expected to pronounce on the popularity of recipient colonies, transportation of recruits from the local up-country sub-depots to Calcutta, the wide divergencies in record keeping practices and the need to regularise entries in the emigration registers. An allied responsibility included investigating complaints by emigration authorities in Demerara (British Guiana) with regard to newly arrived immigrants diagnosed with "epilepsy and weak intellect." Pitcher would ascertain whether their hospitalisation immediately on landing stemmed from "arrangements" in up-country recruiting. Besides, he would determine during prolonged depot detention whether cash advances to inmates might be substituted for daily rations.[18]

Pitcher, an 'honest' reporter, toured largely by rail and horse drawn carriage various recruiting districts in the North-Western Provinces and Oudh from March to June 1882, and gathered first hand information on the impact of immigration in a region which was becoming increasingly popular for Colonial Agents. He inspected the sub-depots of various importing colonies, examined emigration registers and pinpointed discrepancies, interviewed sub-agents, returned emigrants, District Commissioners, Deputy Collectors who were principally responsible for registration, District Superintendents of Police and others. In addition, he detailed the physical and sanitary conditions of depots and noted complaints of recruiters with regard to obstacles in the recruiting process, especially the role of *zamindars* and the police. He even alluded to land availability for purchase by returned emigrants, and emphasised the advantages of recruitment by returned emigrants.

Pitcher submitted a detailed Report to the Government of the North-Western Provinces and Oudh in June 1882.[19] The authorities were favourably impressed and commended him for being "thoroughly practical" and for pinpointing "the actual needs and feelings" of the labouring classes. They considered his various suggestions "valuable and well considered" both in terms of fostering colonial emigration and identifying various obstacles in the recruiting process. The Indian Government's profound satisfaction with the Report and confidence in Pitcher was even reflected in a recommendation that he could undertake similar investigations in Bengal.

The general tenor of Pitcher's Report was that government officers should "directly" encourage emigration, a suggestion made five years earlier by Lord Salisbury but rejected by Indian authorities. Pitcher was thoroughly convinced of the advantages of colonial emigration: "It is pretty universally admitted, and by none more so than by returned emigrants, that even if a man here and there does embark under a deception, he is almost sure to find his opportunities far better than they would have been had he remained in Hindustan."[20] Sir Alfred Lyall, the 'scholarly' Lieutenant-Governor of the North Western Provinces and Oudh, however, was decidedly cautious, echoing the same sentiments of the Government of India:

> There is some reason to fear that this might easily be misinterpreted by those classes to whom such counsel would be addressed, into the notion that the Government is anxious to export its surplus population, and that this rumour might be expanded by a suspicious and ignorant people into some misapprehension of the designs of the Government, leading possibly to mischievous results.[21]

Lyall, who served during the Mutiny of 1857 which rocked the very foundations of the British Raj, was conscious of the impact of fear and rumour on the minds of the uneducated Indian masses prone to view with suspicion every act of the British. Besides, he was not convinced of the advantages of emigration to Indian villagers as Pitcher had implied. He preferred internal migration and suggested that Indians be encouraged to populate vast tracts of uncultivated land to boost sparse population. Therefore, while government officers would endeavour to remove unnecessary obstacles in the recruiting process and ensure legitimate enlistment, the whole transaction should be a matter between the recruiter and the emigrant who was expected to act on a rational calculation of his own economic interests. Indeed, this laissez faire attitude was in harmony with the Indian Government's position on colonial emigration.

Nevertheless, Lyall agreed with Pitcher that Indian women, especially those who were widowed or destitute, had been deserted by their husbands or had tarnished characters, could benefit from an overseas sojourn. He observed:

> A very large proportion of the women who now emigrate are persons who have been turned out of their homes, or have lost their friends by famine or pestilence; and many of them are when they are recruited in a state of extreme destitution and wretchedness. A considerable number of them are of Hindu parentage who have, under the stress of circumstances, become Muhammadans. Further, in the North-Western Provinces and Oudh there are 3,622,107 widows, of whom no less than 3,145,847 are Hindus.[22]

The existing circumstances convinced Lyall that no harm would entail in relaxing medical examination rules since Indian women "would benefit as much or more than the men by emigration." To facilitate emigration, Lyall touted the employment of female recruiters, physical improvements in depots and better accommodation and appropriate clothing for inmates. He advised that while government officers should exercise vigilance against abduction and fraudulent recruitment of women, it was "unnecessary and inadvisable" to mount police enquiries in all cases of suspected recruiting irregularities. Careful questioning by registration officers could, he averred, reveal cases of impropriety. The Lieutenant-Governor was convinced that systematic inspection and supervision of registration would probably prevent "any unreasonableness" on the part of emigration officers.[23]

An allied emigration issue which Pitcher addressed was the importance of improved communication between emigrants resident in the colonies and friends and relatives in India as a means of promoting emigration. Pitcher recommended strongly that postage rates be reduced to the "lowest practicable rate," correspondence by postcard be stimulated by "judicious pressure," and a less complicated system of remittances be introduced. Lauding these timely suggestions, Lyall seemed convinced that they could be implemented in India through a thorough registration process, and the establishment of a special liaison department in terms of tracing emigrants and forwarding remittances promptly and safely. As regards the estates of deceased emigrants in the colonies, Lyall wanted colonial governments to assume some responsibility in communicating expeditiously such information to India.[24]

A fascinating aspect of the Report was Pitcher's candid interviews with several emigrants who returned to their respective villages with small fortunes. Ganga Din Misr, for example, spent eight years in Demerara and returned to Lucknow with 500 *rupees*. He invested in land and cattle, paid off his wife's liabilities and settled down.[25] Three other returnees spent between 12 and 13 years each in Trinidad. They did not amass wealth but exaggerated prevailing conditions in the island: "Hindustan, a country of thieves and liars, while in Trinidad every one is honest and tells the truth... Magistrates very just, and do not favour Creoles more than Indians (Creoles pronounced kirwal). No obstacle to letter-writing beyond the rates of postage."[26]

The returnee, Khan Muhammad, was a conspicuous example of success and an excellent advertisement to emigration. A Punjabi and former police cavalry *sowar* during the Mutiny, Muhammad left his wife and son and emigrated to Demerara in 1862. He spent 18 years, made a fortune, received several commendations for tact and industry, married again and returned with his second wife and family in 1881. He bought '10 ploughs of land' in his native village, settled his wife there and began a search for his first family. He wanted to establish a sub-agency as he was convinced that he could recruit more successfully than current sub-agents. Pitcher affirmed: "I talked with him for a long time, and found him in his common sense and independent way of thinking far more European than native. He had a large silver medal presented to him by his employers and engraved with a flattering testimonial, of which he was proud."[27]

Kanpur to Kolkata is divided principally into two main segments. The first, the Report proper with crucial recommendations, and Appendices providing significant statistical data and other relevant information, was structured in accordance with official instructions coupled with "additional points of discussion and interest."[28] The second is his copious Diary kept during the entire duration of his tour of duty. It not only complements the Report but also provides invaluable information on depot accommodation and physical conditions, the sub-agencies, returned emigrants, railway accommodation to Calcutta and the trauma of families left behind in Village India. Although not part of his mandate, Pitcher also commented on various provisions of the

INTRODUCTION

Indian Emigration Bill of 1883. His incisive observations, however, were largely for the consumption of Indian authorities and are excluded from this study.

The minor editorial changes made in both Pitcher's Report and Diary, particularly in relation to punctuation, paragraphing and writing style, are geared primarily to ensure uniformity and to preserve originality. Even the spelling of certain Indian terms remains unaltered despite the fact that they are spelt differently in the Report and in the Diary. Concomitantly, Pitcher utilises a significant number of Indian terms which necessitate the inclusion of an extended Glossary. Furthermore, since Indian recruits comprised different caste groups in the Indian hierchical structure, I have appended a list of castes and their occupations extracted from the 1881 Population Census of India. These necessary inclusions will, hopefully, make the text clearer and more readable especially for those unfamiliar with their roots or the subject matter.

NOTES

1. Hugh R. Tinker, *A New System of Slavery. The Export of Indian Labour Overseas 1830-1920*. (London: Oxford University Press, 1974), p. 56.
2. For a list see P. Saha, *Emigration of Indian Labour, 1834-1900*. (New Delhi: People's Publishing House, 1970), p. 79.
3. See Govt. of India to Secy. of State for India, no. 15, 3 May 1877. India Emigration Proceedings (I.E.P.), Sept. 1879, File 7.
4. Ibid.
5. See H.N.D. Beyts to Govt. of Bengal, no. 11, 13 April 1861. Bengal Emigration Proceedings (B.E.P.), Aug. 1861, 3.
6. For a detailed discussion of Beyts' recommendation and remarks by Colonial Emigration Agents and the Govt. of Bengal see B.E.P., Feb. 1862, 9. See also B. Mangru, *Benevolent Neutrality. Indian Government Policy and Labour Migration to British Guiana, 1854-1884*. (London: Hansib, 1988), pages 87-88.
7. See Act XIII of 1864, articles 30, 41-43.
8. See Mangru, p. 120. Also Tinker, pp. 126-127.
9. C.O. 319/55. Colonial Office to India Office, 2 Sept. 1871.
10. See West India Committee Reports, 1872-1877.
11. For details of the drafting of this dispatch, see Tinker, pp. 253-254.
12. For a summary of the various responses, see Mangru, pp. 207-214.
13. Lord Salisbury to Govt. of India, no. 39, 24 March 1875. B.E.P. Nov. 1875, File 61.
14. Govt. of India to Secretary of State for India, no. 15, 3 May 1877. I.E.P. Sept. 1879, File 17.
15. See Report of the Protector of Emigrants, 1879-1880.
16. The Bill became Act XXI of 1883.
17. Govt. of India to Govt. of the North Western Provinces and Oudh, no. 217, 16 Oct. 1882. I.E.P. Feb. 1883, 3.
18. Govt. of the North Western Provinces & Oudh to Govt. of India, no. 1726, 25 Sept. 1882. I.E.P. Feb. 1883, file 55.
19. Pitcher to Govt. of the North Western Provinces & Oudh, 17 June 1882. I.E.P. Feb. 1883.

20. Pitcher's Report, para. 46.
21. Govt. of the North-Western Provinces and Oudh to Govt. of India, no. 1726, 25 Sept. 1882. I.E.P. Feb. 1883.
22. Ibid.
23. Ibid.
24. Ibid.
25. Pitcher, Diary, 16 March 1882.
26. Ibid., 10 April 1882.
27. Ibid., 19 April 1882.
28. Pitcher to Govt. of North-Western Provinces and Oudh, 17 June 1882. I.E.P., Feb. 1883.

Report on System of Recruiting Labourers for the Colonies, 1882

By D.G. PITCHER

1. As a step preliminary to my commencing the proposed enquiry into the existing system of emigration, I was directed to attend at the Revenue and Agricultural Office in Calcutta, where, on the 24th February, I met the Protector of Emigrants, Bengal, the Agents in charge of the various emigration depots, and other officers interested in the subject. I further visited the depots, and so was enabled to acquaint myself with some of the details of the system, together with the opinions and needs of the Agents.

2. Returning to Lucknow to await further orders, I received, on the 6th March, permission to commence work.

3. A well-known result of emigration is that every year witnesses shiploads of emigrants returning, many of whom possess considerable sums of money.

It is within my experience, from conversation with various returned emigrants, to say that colonial life, more often than not, works a very remarkable change in rendering them far more wide-awake and independent, and less inclined to bow the neck to caste dictation, than are those who are untravelled.

The wealth of the returned emigrant often excites the cupidity of his neighbours, and, unless he can soon find a good investment, the attempts to get money from him under various pretexts, such as caste dinners, &c., and even by theft, become burdensome, and so, many re-emigrate after a few months, fairly disillusionised with Hindustan.

4. It was with a view to providing a fair investment for the capital of this class that, in 1878, I suggested the possibility of inducing returned emigrants possessed of capital to settle down in communities on available waste lands. On the other hand, Colonel Mac Andrew (late

Commissioner of Sitapur) has for some few years been elaborating a scheme for attracting small capitalists to take up certain waste lands in the Kheri district of Oudh, a scheme commonly known as the Kutna Valley scheme. To find the eligible capitalist had so far been a practical difficulty.

5. As one plan seemed to complement the other, I communicated with Major Erskine, the present Commissioner of Sitapur, and, in reply, received a telegram to join his camp, which happened then to be close to the waste lands in question.

6. Accordingly, I gave over charge at Lucknow on the 6th, and joined Major Erskine's camp at Mohamdi via Shahjahanpur on the morning of the 7th.

There I had the advantage of discussing details, perusing plans together with a bulky correspondence, and of viewing the locality of the proposed settlements in company with the Commissioner, Deputy Commissioner, and Executive Engineer.

The locations were unfit for immediate settlement, the first indispensable preliminary of a masonry well for drinking purposes to be sunk for each village being still in progress, while the lots required surveying and marking out, and the terms of the leases had to be settled.

7. Before I left the camp, arrangements were made by the Deputy Commissioner for pushing on the well-sinking and allotment survey, and the terms of the leases were fixed. I subsequently forwarded a sketch of these terms to the Emigration Agents in Calcutta for communication to any emigrants who might seem inclined to invest in land. The reply was to the effect that those spoken to wished to visit their homes first. There has, so far, been barely time to allow of any coming forward, and the season is now too far advanced for settling operations; but, by the commencement of next working season, matters will be in a more forward state for testing the practical value of the scheme, which, if successful, can be extended to some 7,000 acres in the Gonda district, and to hundreds of thousands of acres in the Central Provinces. It is, if I may so suggest, a matter which, when my present duties terminate, may well be taken up by the Agricultural Department.

REPORT ON SYSTEM OF RECRUITING LABOURERS FOR THE COLONIES, 1882

8. Returning to Lucknow via Kheri and Sitapur by the 11th, I found work in visiting the Lucknow depots, and in inspecting the Lucknow registers, until the 14th, when I moved into camp in the Mohanlalganj *tahsil* of the Lucknow district. The registers showed that a great number of people had emigrated from this *tahsil* during the scarcity of 1877-78, added to which, from having formerly held charge of the *tahsil*, I was personally well acquainted with most of the *zamindars,* and had, therefore, the more chance of obtaining their confidence and of eliciting trustworthy information. It had been my intention to march on through the Rae Bareli, Sultanpur, and other populous districts eastwards; but on the 19th March, the hot winds set in with such violence and appearance of continuousness, that it seemed sheer waste of time remaining in tents, a prisoner practically for the greater part of each day; so, on the 21st, I struck camp and thenceforth travelled by rail or *dak.*

9. Short as the time spent amongst the villagers was, it enabled me to appreciate some general points of the system quite as much as a more extended tour might have done; still there was so much both interesting and instructive, that I gave up further marching with very sincere reluctance. As shown in my diary, I found wives who had long supposed their husbands dead of starvation and who only learnt through me that the husband had emigrated; parents who had given up their children as lost, until I was able to assure them to the contrary, and to make them happy by promising to write letters for them: other wives who knew that their husbands had emigrated, but (for in some cases 18 years) had vainly waited for news, and knew not whether the emigrant was alive or dead.

10. Leaving Lucknow again on the night of the 21st. I visited Cawnpore, from whence and from Agra had come the loudest complaints of police interference. After visiting the depots, inspecting the registers, and communicating with the Collector, 1 returned to Lucknow, and then visited in turn the following stations; Rae Bareli, Fyzabad, Gonda, Basti, Gorakhpur, Azamgarh, Jaunpur, Benares, Allahabad, Fatehpur, Allahabad again, and then to Lucknow to collect my letters, and to obtain further information from the sub-agents as to the depots above Cawnpore. A residue of friction between recruiters and the police at the latter station compelled a second visit to it, from whence I went to

Etawah, Mainpuri, Agra, Muttra, Aligarh, Moradabad, Shahjahanpur, Lucknow again, Bahraich and Bara Banki.

11. This list includes nearly all those stations at which active recruiting has been carried on during the months of March and April, and includes every station, regarding the conduct of business at which recruiters have lately brought complaints. To some extent my enquiries have been limited by the fact, that recruiting for the French and British West Indian Colonies and British Guiana, which colonies collectively take by far the largest number of recruits, was at a standstill for the months of March and April. Hence, I was left to discover what I could amongst the recruits for Fiji and Natal. Again, several of the sub-agents are Jews, who, when I was visiting the stations from Gorakhpur to Allahabad, were keeping the feast of the Passover at Calcutta or elsewhere, leaving only recruiters in charge.

12. My method has been:

(a) To inspect the registration registers at each station, noting the divergences in practice, which proved to be rather considerable, and judging, so far as was possible, how far the complaints by the recruiters of indiscriminate rejection of recruits was borne out. I also endeavoured to trace from the registers the existence of the practice, alleged by some Magistrates to be common, of recruiters registering in one district the recruits collected in another.
(b) To visit each local depot, inspect the sanitary and other arrangements, and, unattended, to converse with the recruits, occasionally by the hour together, as to their general impressions of the business on which they were bound.
(c) To cross-question the sub-agents and recruiters as to their previous modes of living, length of service, &c., and to ascertain their difficulties and grievances, noting such suggestions as they might have to offer.
(d) To examine the records of cases where complaints against recruiters had formed the subject of Magisterial enquiry.
(e) To discover returned emigrants when possible, and to elicit from them their experiences and suggestions.
(f) To elicit from natives of various grades any public opinion that might exist on the subject of emigration.

(g) To discuss with district officers such matters as appeared to interfere with legitimate recruiting.

13. Having thus attempted to sketch out the way in which I have worked to obtain information, I will proceed to reply to each head of my instructions in detail.

I. To ascertain by visiting local depots how arrangements are carried on, and whether they are properly managed

14. Recruiting may be divided into two systems, that maintained by the Trinidad Agency, and that by the Demerara Agency, respectively.

15. Under the Trinidad systems the sub-agents receive for the most part a monthly salary, in addition to a certain commission on each recruit payable on embarkation. For this commission, as the agents prefer to call it, rather than contract, the sub-agent undertakes every expense connected with the coolie up to the day of his entry into the Calcutta depot, including such items as hire of depots, registration fees, railway fare, food, and the pay of the up-country establishments of recruiters, writers, and *chaprassis*. Exceptions are the recruiter's license fees and fees for medical examination, which are borne by the agent. To the recruit, while in the Calcutta depot, cash is given for the purchase of food, and each is allowed to cook for himself after his own fashion. Up-country, sometimes cash is given and sometimes food, but each man is allowed to cook his own food.

16. The Demerara Agency pays no fixed salary to the sub-agents, but pays, on the whole, a higher rate of commission, and gives at the end of the season a bonus per 100 coolies to such sub-agents as may have worked well.

Recruiters have to pay the license fee themselves.

In the Calcutta depot food is served out on the *bhandara* system - that is to say, it is cooked in large boilers by Brahman cooks and then served out - rice is supplied in this way, whereas the coolie of the North-Western Provinces and Oudh is, as a rule, a flour-eater rather than a rice-eater.

17. All the sub-agents up-country have the recruiters under them. Sometimes the sub-agent holds a recruiter's license, but as often not. Apparently, beyond occasionally seeing a recruiter when the latter may happen to visit Calcutta in charge of a batch of coolies, the agents have little knowledge of them, and no real control. It is the sub-agent who in practice appoints and dismisses them.

A sub-agent may suspect a recruiter of taking coolies to some depot other than the one to which he is engaged, or there is a quarrel between the two on the subject of accounts; in either case the sub-agent may write to Calcutta and get the recruiter's license cancelled. I found two cases where recruiters were under suspension, as it were, by sub-agents, on what one may call private disagreements. The recruiter in such a case usually betakes himself to another depot where he finds employment as a *chaprassi.*

18. Just as the sub-agent works on commission, so, in the majority of cases, do the recruiters work for the subagents on commission. Occasionally 1 found recruiters working on monthly pay.

19. As Appendices I and II are annexed the forms of agreement:

(1) between the agent and sub-agent:
(2) between the sub-agent and recruiter.

It will be seen that in both cases responsibility is carefully fended off until it rests with the recruiter alone. And a very curious point about it is that, while the agent always pays a higher sum for women than for men, under the supposition that women are so much more difficult to obtain, the subagent, not unfrequently, pays to the recruiter the same sum for women as for men, or with very little difference.

20. Below the recruiter again are *arkatis,* or unlicensed men, who bring in coolies to the recruiter, but with whom, of course, no enforceable contract can exist. I have heard it asserted that village *chaukidars* and *patwaris* are occasionally not above turning a few *rupees* in this way, getting rid of troublesome characters at the same time, but have had no proof.

21. *Arkatis* are not universally employed, but rather in such places only where recruiters are few and the chances of obtaining coolies good. The transaction with the *arkatis* must be a cash one, and the recruiter can only afford to engage them when his margin of profit is fairly good.

22. Women are undoubtedly employed near large towns as *arkatis*, such women being generally connected in some way either with the recruiter or with one of the *chaprassis* of the depot.

23. The *arkati's* business is, I believe, solely limited to introducing coolies to recruiters within a few hours of their first meeting with the coolies, and I have failed to discover that they go about districts collecting gangs of men under pretence of giving them work at the under station, as has been suggested. If such a practice ever existed, I do not think that it exists now. I look on the idea of recruiters carrying coolies about from district to district before registering them with a view to involving the coolies in debt as equally apocryphal.

24. To most depots is attached a writer to keep accounts, who is unlicensed.

25. Every depot has several unlicensed *chaprassis* who look after the coolies, go with the *chalans* or batches of registered coolies to Calcutta, and go out with the recruiter to fairs, &c. So soon as the recruiter has engaged a few men, he sends them to the depot in charge of one of his *chaprassis*, remaining himself to enlist, if possible, some more coolies.

26. The sub-agent's contract with the recruiter usually makes the latter entirely responsible for the coolie's good faith, and his expenses, up to delivery into the train. The expenses of feeding, lodging, and registering all coolies who previous to the train starting may die, desert, refuse to go, or who may be rejected either by the medical officer, or by the officer conducting registration, all falls on the contracting recruiter. Casualties occurring between the station of delivery up-country and embarkation from the Calcutta depot fall on the sub-agent.

27. It must be admitted that this system is likely to act powerfully in securing from the recruiter and sub-agent great caution in the selection

of recruits. It further secures an ample guarantee for good treatment of the recruits while in depot or when journeying.

28. There does not appear to be any regular scale laid down as to the food to be supplied, but the coolies have always assured me of their entire satisfaction in this respect, save on one occasion, where some coolies who had received *ghi* at Muttra complained of not getting the same quantity while halting for a couple of days or so at Lucknow, and in the same batch two nursing women pleaded for an allowance of milk. It is manifestly to the recruiter's interest that the coolie shall remain not only satisfied, but in good condition; and I found cases where men in bad condition were being carefully fed up to a presentable appearance. Tobacco, *pawn,* and such small luxuries are allowed. In one depot I found two coolies who had been upwards of four months there, recovering from fever, and who assured me that they had had all they required in the shape of food and medicine. In another I found a man who had lived free at one sub-agency some six months, and was then completing the year at another, but whose ribs still showed unpleasantly. He was evidently too comfortable to think of moving, and as he volubly declared his readiness to go to any part of the known world at any moment, the recruiter seemed somewhat puzzled with the investment.

29. The local depots are ordinary native houses, and vary greatly in internal arrangements. At some few the coolies are allowed to wander in and out all day without let or hindrance, at others egress is only allowed under restriction. I am bound to state, however, that *bandish,* as the system of maintaining a guard over the door is termed, is maintained most strictly at those places where the interference of the police and of the townspeople is most complained of. At Fyzabad, where the coolies in the Trinidad depot seemed free at any time to go where they liked, even to returning to their villages to bring in their families, there is no sort of friction between the police and the recruiters.

30. These defects are usually found:

    (1)   want of cleanliness
    (2)   want of room

(3) want of separate accommodation for married couples and single women.

In the Trinidad and Demerara depots (representing Fiji and Natal respectively) at Fyzabad alone did I find such separate accommodation maintained as I could thoroughly approve of.

31. The system of giving several recruiters working in the same district separate contracts naturally leads to keen competition, and in two or three large towns I found, in the place of a large central depot, several recruiters working under one sub-agent, but each with his own small depot, keeping his recruits like fowls in a pen, and, as a result, neither decency, nor cleanliness, nor room.

32. That the hire of a house for a depot should form part of a sub-agent's or recruiter's contract is clearly a mistake, as tempting to undue economy.

33. Occasionally the sub-agent gives the sub-contract to some *baniah* or other unlicensed man, who pays the recruiter monthly wages.

34. In one depot, under an unlicensed sub-contractor of this description, I found at the time of my visit a man in charge whose license had been cancelled some time ago. He admitted that the sub-contractor and the licenced recruiter had been absent some eight or nine days trying to get money from the sub-agent. A *baniah*, who supplied food daily to the depot, said he was doing so on credit; he was owed Rs. 50 and did not personally know the licensed recruiter, a fact which rather confirmed what a rival recruiter told me, viz., that no recruiter had been to this depot for six weeks. There were three coolies present, two men and one woman, while there were six other women, of whom at least three were admittedly kept women, and the others of doubtful respectability. These women belonged to a number of men residing in the house, nominally as relatives of the sub-contractor, but probably as *arkatis*. The house itself was most unsuitable and dirty, and to crown all there was a child in the house covered with small-pox. Altogether, had every depot in the province but this one been in good order, this alone would have demonstrated the necessity for supervision of some sort or kind, and the establishment of rules to insure:

(1) cleanliness
(2) sufficient room for the average number of coolies composing a *chalan*, which varies somewhat according to the district
(3) the exclusion of cases of contagious disease
(4) the exclusion of all women not coolies, save such women married to recruiters or *chaprassis,* for whose residence special permission may have been obtained, such permission not to include *pardah* women, as the excuse of *pardah* prevents free access to every part of the depot
(5) accommodation for single women and married people apart from the single men, such separate accommodation to be in charge of a female depot servant
(6) the regulation by register and license of every one attached to the depot, and the rigid exclusion of all not attached
(7) That neither sub-agent nor recruiter leave the district without first giving notice of their reasons for doing so to the officer in charge.

35. While advocating the proper regulation and supervision of depots, I still think that care will have to be exercised lest officers be carried away by exalted ideas of the extent of accommodation and sanitation necessary, and thus land the Agencies in uncalled for expense by insisting on modes and methods suitable only for European troops.

36. There is a matter of clothing, which I think may be improved. From November to February the nights are often bitterly cold, and I am sure that the Agencies would find their service more attractive if it became the rule to serve out to each coolie a new blanket so soon as registered, and allow him to take this blanket on shipboard with him, as part of the regulation allowance. This would scarcely be an additional expense, as country blankets can be procured much cheaper up-country than in Calcutta. Many of the women enter the depots in a garment of filthy rags, which can hardly be said to clothe them. A new *dhoti* to

each woman would go far to diminish the chances of disease germs being conveyed on shipboard, and at the same time render recruiting more popular with women.

37. Sub-agents and recruiters generally ascribe all their difficulties to the police and to the action of the Magistracy, but a few honestly admit that a large share of their difficulties is attributable to the rivalry and competition existing everywhere between the sub-agencies working for different Agencies in the same district, while occasionally sub-agencies of the same Agency are found set in competition.

38. This very natural result is sometimes further stimulated by the Agencies offering different rates of commission at the same place. In Allahabad for instance, while the sub-agent for Fiji was receiving commission at the rate of Rs. 18 per man and Rs. 28 per woman, the Natal sub-agent was receiving Rs. 22 per man and Rs. 33 per woman. Then, again, one colony offers superior terms to the others. Mauritius offers what to a lazy man is tempting, viz., regular monthly wages, while Demerara can only offer daily pay: the French colonies can promise a free return passage after five years, where Trinidad can only promise the free passage after 10 years, and so on. It is too much to expect perhaps, but it seems a great pity, that some general scheme for all the colonies cannot be agreed on, so that, other things being equal, the rates of pay for sub-agents and the rates of commission might be equalised at all stations, and that the terms of service and pay in the colonies might be made to accord in some way to the drawbacks which are undoubtedly to be found in some colonies as compared to others.

39. Until some equalisation of terms is effected these rivalries are bound to continue; but with the depots under official supervision there will be, it may be fairly hoped, some mitigation of rancour.

40. 1 have taken some little pains to ascertain which system was the one most popular amongst recruiters, and found that the Trinidad Agency had the preference in the fixed salaries of sub-agents, payment by the Agency of license fees of recruiters, and in the depot arrangements at Calcutta for coolies' food; which latter affects recruiters, inasmuch as that the coolie, if dissatisfied, is the more likely

to desert. Taking them all round, I must give the palm of superior management up-country to the Trinidad depots and sub-agents.

41. If, then, a few first steps, as taken by the Trinidad agency towards paying salaries and fixed charges, are found to produce beneficial results, it seems plainly indicated that a move may safely be made along the whole line in the same direction, and that the contract system should be narrowed down as far as may be practicable.

II. To make enquiries as to the recruiters employed, of what class they are, and what is their character, and as far as possible what is their method of recruiting

42. The class from which recruiters spring is that which supplies *sepoys, chaprassis*, and domestic servants. I found men who had previously been employed as bearers, *khidmatgars,* cavalry *sowars,* infantry and police *sepoys, cutcherry chaprassis*, and so on; while some had been recruiters from their youth upwards. Very few of them could read or write, those who had sub-contracts paying a writer to keep accounts for them. Here and there were men whose manner and way of speaking would lead any judge of native character to distrust them; but taking the men as a body, I have come to the conclusion that, particularly in view of the difficulties under which they work, they have been somewhat unjustly maligned.

Generally they are residents either of the district in which employed or of some large town in the province, and many of them have been from 15 to 20 years at the work without getting into trouble.

The amount of ridicule and abuse which recruiters have to stand from the *bazaar,* the undoubted fact that their occupation is much looked down upon by the well-to-do classes, the strong antagonism with which they frequently have to cope both in the police and in the district offices, the absence of any sort of controlling authority to promptly punish or to give support.

All the above disadvantages tend to injure the self-respect and esteem of these men; added to which, I consider the practice of employing them on commission to some extent demoralising. It is plenty of money one month and debt the next, tending to foster in uneducated men a gambling and reckless spirit. "It is of no use denying," said a recruiter to me, "that many recruiters are gamblers and debauchees, and are considerably in debt with the sub-agent" - a state of things which suits the sub-agents, as rendering the recruiters more dependent.

43. At page 8 of his report for 1879-80 the Protector of Emigrants, Calcutta, remarks:

"The number of recruiting licenses granted during 1879-80 was large in comparison with the number granted in 1878-79, but, as may be noticed in the following table, the percentage of licenses cancelled was not by any means so large as that of the previous years. This result was due partly to the extensive weeding out during 1878-79 of all doubtful characters, and partly to the more sparing recourse during 1879-80 to the extreme measure of cancellation for comparatively venial offences. In some instances licenses were temporarily withdrawn pending the enquiry into alleged or suspected misconduct, and were subsequently restored after reproof or warning, when the offences had been ascertained to be of a nature not sufficient to warrant permanent forfeiture of license. For, as was submitted in the communication marginally noted, excepting cases of a serious nature, when it is simply out of the question to think of renewing license, there are numerous instances, I believe, in which the cancellation or permanent refusal of a license to one who has hitherto been a fairly-well conducted recruiter ultimately does more harm than good. Their formal exclusion from the work of recruitment does not necessarily ensure their real exclusion from it. If the one certainly ensured the other, the cancellation of licenses would indeed be a most efficient mode of getting rid of many offenders, but unfortunately it is not so. On the other hand, the disadvantages of resorting too freely to the cancellation of licences are sufficient to make one hesitate before recommending the permanent exclusion of those who have already been connected with recruiting operations, and have hitherto conducted themselves with tolerable regard to the requirements of the law. Such men when excluded for comparatively minor offences necessarily carry away with them not only much knowledge of the work, and many useful experiences which would deter them from committing errors that the less experienced are likely to commit, but they retain also in most instances probably a direct money interest in the work which, therefore, they cannot afford to give up. The result is that, though ostensibly disconnected, they secretly maintain their connection; and, by swelling the ranks of a host of unlicensed recruiters who skilfully manage to keep out of sight and to evade the law, they ultimately tend to increase the very evil that their exclusion was intended to diminish. Nor, indeed, do the fresh men who take the place of those who are shut out give any promise of doing in the course of time any better than their predecessors, who belong socially to the same class and differ in all probability only in having been detected."

In the above remarks, after enquiring into several cases of licenses being either confiscated or reported for cancellation, I very cordially agree. To secure good recruiters a license must not be confiscated by the Magistrates too lightly, and, whenever it may be considered necessary to resort to such an extreme measure, it should only be carried out on a regular proceeding showing the evidence, and the judgment formed thereon, and from such judgment I would allow an appeal to the Commissioner.

44. Commenting on that chapter of the new Emigration Bill in which is proposed an increased scale of punishment for offences by recruiters, the Consular Agent at Karikal remarks:

"I am of opinion that the innovation of imprisonment is not an improvement. We are too much inclined perhaps to think and act as if all recruiters were rogues. But our object should be to raise their status and induce more respectable men to take up this occupation; and this object will certainly not be attained as long as a respectable native, who is inclined to invest his money in this trade, finds that one of its alternatives is 'imprisonment for a term which may extend to six months.'"

With something in the nature of a fixed salary combined with head money, or with a less intricate contract, and a knowledge that their operations will be the subject of closer local interest and inspection, I think there is fair room for the expectation that recruiters, as a class, may be improved.

45. Appendix III shows the number of coolies who have been registered in the North-Western Provinces and Oudh during the past four years. During this period 262 recruiters were licensed. Of 28 cases instituted against recruiters, 10 resulted in the cancellation of licenses. Some of the convictions were, in my humble opinion, scarcely sustainable, but even then, I think few will say that the return discloses such an amount of crime amongst this class as to call for increased penalties.

46. Reverting to the greatly increased penalties which have been provided for recruiters in the new Bill, it seems somewhat strange that we should devise such stringent measures in connection with a scheme which at other times we extol as being philanthropical. It is pretty universally admitted, and by none more so than by returned emigrants, that even if a man here and there does embark under a deception, he is almost sure to find his opportunities far better than they would have been had he remained in Hindustan.

Of Demerara coolies, in 1860, Anthony Trollope wrote: "It appears to me that these men could not be treated with more tenderness unless they were put separately, each under his own glass-case with a piece of velvet on which to lie. In England we know of no such treatment for field labourers; I think I may venture to say that no labourers in any country are so cared for, so closely protected, so certainly saved from the usual wants and sorrows incident to the labouring classes. The planter who has allotted to him such labour becomes almost as much subject to Government inspection as though his estate were Government property."

Of the coolies in Trinidad, Canon Kingsley wrote in 1871: "On the Monday morning there was a great parade. All the coolies were to come up to see the Governor, and a long dark line of people arrived up the lawn, the women in their gaudiest muslins and some of them in cotton velvet jackets of the richest colours. There were bangles and jewels among them in plenty. A merrier, healthier, shrewder-looking party I have seldom seen. Complaints there were none, all seemed to look on the squire as a father, and each face brightened when he spoke to them by name. The pleasure of the men at the whole ceremony was very noticeable and very pleasant. Well fed, well cared for, well taught (when they will allow themselves to be so), and with a local medical man appointed for their special benefit, coolies under such a master ought to be, and are, prosperous and happy." And again:

"The coolie women sat in groups on the grass like live flower beds of the most splendid and yet harmonious hues. As for jewels of gold as well as silver there were many there."

That the condition and prospects of a recruit of the army or navy of England is increased by his enlisting to any parallel extent is not universally admitted. Yet there, all is considered fair play in recruiting so long as the man's consent can be gained, and small blame attaches to the recruiter. Expediency is at the root of the matter.

47. The ideal method of recruiting is that of recruiters going about amongst the towns and villages and enlisting people at their homes or near them. I can certainly say that, until 1 entered up this enquiry, I conceived this to be the method. The emigration correspondence shows that other officers hold to a similar idea when they write of recruiters 'running about from district to district picking up a few men here and a few men there and eventually taking them to be registered in some other district' and thereupon raise a structure of argument in favour of restricting registration to the residents of the district only.

48. I am convinced that, as a matter of fact, recruiters very seldom if ever recruit in any district but that for which they are licensed. The North-Western Provinces and Oudh are quartered out, so to speak, amongst recruiters, and the acute rivalry to which I have before alluded is an effectual check against one man encroaching on the district of another. Nor does the system of contract admit of the recruiter going any considerable distance from his local depot. As soon as he had collected a few men, he would either have to travel back to the depot with them himself, or keep a number of *chaprassis* with him to convoy away batches, which would be expensive.

49. Occasionally a recruiter may pay a visit to some large town or mela at a distance from head-quarters, but, ordinarily their procedure is to station themselves on the main arteries of traffic, just outside the town, particularly at wells and near bridges, where travellers stop to

rest and drink, and to accost those who are wandering in search of work. The recruiter, no doubt, sets forth his proposal in highly-coloured language just as an auctioneer does, and very possibly finds in many a tired man fleeing from debt, or home trouble, very plastic material; but, from specimens I have seen myself in the depots, I am convinced that, even if stated in the most simple fashion, the prospect of good and sufficient food with complete rest from work for some five or six months, with certain wages for fair work to follow, in a congenial climate free from famine and cholera, must come like a godsend to many a weary soul. No small proportion of these wanderers have left their own province or district under the shadow of some misdeed. If, however, there is one thing which the returned emigrant harps on more than another, it is the effect of emigration in converting dishonest into honest men: in the colonies, say they, a man can so easily satisfy his hunger that there is no temptation to steal. Probably also there is greater certainty of detection. So men remain honest who in a struggle for existence would be thieves. A District Superintendent of Police assured me lately that, during the cold weather, he had taken some trouble to enquire in their villages as to the present mode of life of men who had been convicted, and was surprised to find how many had emigrated.

50. It is better for the country, and for those men themselves, that they should have the opportunity afforded in a new country, and in the absence of temptation, of becoming good citizens. District and police officers should recognise that, in this matter, the recruiter is rather an ally than a foe. The district in which of all others I found recruiting in the most satisfactory state, the depots best managed, and the best class of recruits, was one where both District Superintendent of Police and District Officers had openly recommended emigration in the villages when on their cold weather tours.

51. This shows clearly how very cosmopolitan is the character of the recruiting at any particular place. To insist too closely on knowing why a native of Bombay comes to be enlisted at Lucknow is merely to hatch lies; to refuse to register at Fyzabad a widow from Rajputana, who has perhaps expended her last article of property in achieving a pilgrimage to Adjudhia, is, as likely as not, to throw her on the town; to reject a Nepaulese because he does not 'reside in the district' is to

deprive the colonies of one of their best classes of workmen; and, generally speaking, to confine registration in a district to residents of that district only, as so strongly recommended by some officers, would reduce the already insufficient number of recruits by one-half, would vastly increase the expenses of the colonies, and would increase the difficulties of life to thousands of homeless wanderers.

52. Besides frequenting the highways, recruiters find the neighbourhood of large railway stations, *sarais,* fairs, markets, and places of pilgrimage fruitful sources of recruits. So also are the *Sadhabarts* of Benares and Muttra, where pious Hindus distribute food and clothing to the poor.

53. Save in three or four districts, recruiters never visit the outlying villages. For one thing, they are afraid of rough treatment, and for another, unless a man goes with his whole family, his relatives would consider it generally a point of honor not to let him go. In the case of families, if they are in debt, as so many of them are, their removal is obstructed by their creditors. *Zamindars* in many villages object on principle to any removes, fearing that the rate of wages of daily labour may be thereby forced up. Of this I have had instances.

54. One marked feature of emigration for the last few years is the re-emigration of returned emigrants, accompanied by numbers of relatives and friends. An old emigrant of the Jaunpur district returned to Demerara in August, 1881, accompanied by some 70 people (men, women, and children), of his own caste, and all from his own or from neighbouring villages. A returning female emigrant during the past season took with her 19 women. The last entry at Fyzabad before my arrival was that of nine men accompanying a returned emigrant. Similar examples were numerous in the Fyzabad register.

55. Frequently in the depots I have found that the motive for going has been supplied by the accounts received from some returned emigrant neighbour.

56. Such being the case, one would naturally think that sub-agents would mark down returned emigrants at their homes, and then send a

recruiter to that neighbourhood; but no, scarcely a recruiter can be found who can name on the fingers of one hand any old emigrants, and very few who, after years of work, can name any at all.

57. The question has frequently been raised whether returned emigrants would not make good recruiters. I am quite sure that some of them might be so employed with advantage. A Panjabi came to me a short time ago and asked if I could help him to get a license and a sub-agency. He was a fine, independent, frank man, who had spent 18 years in Demerara, from whence he had returned with an excellent character and a large sum of money: and only a few days ago, again, another returned emigrant asked me if I could get him a license. I referred both of these men to the emigration sub-agents, but have not heard of their receiving any encouragement.

58. In truth, the sub-agency business is somewhat of a monopoly, and to a striking extent in the hands of Jews; the want of more supervision up-country is incontrovertible

59. Everywhere recruiters complain very much of the way in which they are insulted at times in the *bazaars*, and of the language and falsehoods with which their recruits are assailed. It has been found necessary to protect the recruiting service in England from similar annoyances by section 98 (4), Army Act, 1881, which renders any one liable, on summary conviction, to a fine not exceeding £20 who shall directly or indirectly interfere with the recruiting service. I venture to submit that a section added to the new Act rendering persons liable to a small penalty, say not exceeding Rs. 10, who shall directly or indirectly interfere with the recruiting service of the colonies, would greatly help to improve the tone of the recruiting class.

III. To ascertain the feeling of the native community on the subject of emigration

60. The feeling of the native community on the subject of emigration is, for the most part, either nil, or a ludicrous distorted image, in which the coolie hangs with his head downward like a flying-fox, or is ground in mills for oil,[1] or is otherwise oppressed by the Briton. In one place

I found an honest belief that China was the destination of all recruits, and that opium was cultivated for a people who had heads like horses and possessed the secret of weaving broad-cloth. The idea of many educated natives still is that recruiting is carried on with the view of forcibly populating certain desert countries the property of the Indian Government, and that the idea of the coolies ever returning is absurd.

61. I asked an educated native gentleman, whose essays in reply to various questions of the Famine Commission found great favour, to oblige me with an essay on emigration. This gentleman, 1 may say, has since emigrated himself to England to study Agriculture, and, as he had been for years in the Educational Department, I took it for granted that he was well informed. His parable however was that the recruit was a "miserable wretch," &c., &c., and was habitually deceived by "very imposing looking fibs."

62. Perhaps the feeling most general to rich and poor, in which even native Deputy Collectors and Inspectors of Police share, is that the coolies are made to eat pork and beef; are deprived of caste in malice afore-thought, and are forcibly converted to Christianity. Recruiters boldly say that such opinions have been communicated to coolies in open court, and the figures for recruiting for one or two districts give some support to the assertion.

63. Perhaps it is this idea which in some degree gives to emigration the bad name it has acquired. A few days ago I received a kindly hint from a native gentleman, under the impression that I had permanently joined the Emigration Department, that various native friends of mine had been heard to express extreme sorrow at my marring a hitherto honorable career by such an act.

64. Now I venture to say boldly, notwithstanding all the weight of opinion in the Blue-books against me, that, in the words of the Secretary of State's Despatch No. 39 dated 24th March, 1875, "there might be a considerable change in the attitude of the Indian Government towards emigration through its officers, by more directly encouraging it than heretofore." Why, when Government attempts to grapple with every other form of ignorance, should it not grapple with this also. It is surely

a greater political danger to allow the beliefs regarding interference with caste, and forcible conversion to Christianity, to remain unchallenged, than to systematically set to work to destroy them? A knowledge of the countries where three-quarters of a million of their fellow-countrymen reside may fairly be considered to be of more importance to school children than the geography of places which no Indian is likely ever to visit, and a descriptive account of the colonies to which coolies proceed might be introduced as a reader in the Government school. If it could but be so arranged that, for the next ten years or so, every coolie returned for a visit to his home when his time came for a free passage, the political gain arising from the information brought back by these people would far outweigh any sort of political danger which may be feared from Government taking an active part in promoting emigration.

IV. To ascertain whether in ordinary years any part of the population is in want of work and whether the labour market is in any part or the recruiting field overstocked

65. The cry that, if Government interests itself more actively than hitherto, emigration will be looked on as an official affair, seems to me rather empty. If my investigations have convinced me of one thing more than another, it is that the line between Government and emigration is as visible to the people at large as the line at the equator, and that the mass of the people have long ceased to regard the Emigration Department as anything but *sarkari*. It is, I venture to think, a mistake to suppose that the people now-a-days will submit quietly to being forced from their homes because some one tells them that it is the wish of the *sarkar*.

65a. In all years, apparently, there is a stream of wanderers along highways converging on large towns from which stream nearly one-half of the total number of recruits is drawn. Amongst recruiters certain towns have a reputation in that way and are known as *nakas*. Cawnpore, Delhi, and Lucknow are great *nakas;* Allahabad, Fyzabad and Benares furnish many recruits from amongst their pilgrims, and Benares from its *sadabarts*. Agra is a great *naka* for people from the Native States. Muttra affords many female recruits, being a favourite place of pilgrimage with women. It would require a more extended local enquiry than I have been able to make to answer this question fully, but I may remark, from the study of many registers, that closer attention to these registers might at times afford useful information.

For instance, during the scarcity of 1877-78 the number of recruits began to rise with the fears of the people; and the influx of people (as shown by the registers) from certain districts in abnormal numbers into other districts might certainly indicate where trouble lay, the more easily if a monthly copy of the registrations in each district were sent to the Agricultural Department and there abstracted for comparison.

66. In some years the labour market suddenly gets overstocked, and with emigration under the care of the Agricultural Department, intimation of the fact could be given to the agents. For instance, the completion of some great public work throws a large number of men out of employ. The completion of the Oudh and Rohilkhand Railway to Moradabad throw whole villages of *kahars* out of employ who had up to that time been earning a livelihood as *palki-bearers*, and terribly those people suffered in 1877-78. The Gonda Babraich Railway in like manner will throw large numbers of boatmen out of employ. The conclusion of the Cabul War has flooded the Panjab with men in want of work, and a recruiter who lately collected a splendid batch of men at Umritsar for Fiji reports that any number of men are procurable there.

Again, a large amount of rain falling in December and January deprives the labouring classes of the wages ordinarily earned at irrigation work, and improves recruiting, while a good harvest and cheap grain necessarily has a contrary effect.

V. Whether the present system of registration admits of any reform, and if so, what better system can be proposed?

67. The present system of registration admits, I think, of considerable reform:

(1) In the absence hitherto of some one to inspect the registers, and thereby to insure one uniform system, all sorts of divergences in procedure have crept in.

(2) The work of examining each coolie apart from the recruiter takes up considerable time. In some large stations, coolies frequently come up in the batches of 100 and more, to register whom properly according to instructions would take a couple of hours. If the work of Magistrates was so easy that on any given day they could easily spare two hours, or even an hour, there would be ground for saying that they are lightly worked; which, however, is certainly not the case. No one, sensible of the great responsibility attaching to judicial decisions, cares to have a trial suddenly interrupted and his attention distracted by the irruption of an evil-smelling crowd, endowed apparently with extraordinary stupidity. The registering officer of experience knows what is before him and inwardly groans. In asking the usual questions, he loses much time who asks them out of the regular order; and to the question "what wages have you been promised" will perhaps get the reply "five years;" and so on: all little matters tending to disturb the temper and to tinge the recruiter with a colour of fraud. I have satisfied myself that the coolie of the depot, like the villager in his native village, when spoken to kindly and in the possession of his self-confidence, has, for the most part, very shrewd ideas as to his own value in the business he is about, and is a very different person to the coolie or villager when in *cutcherry*. Before entering the presence, the coolies have probably had to wait in the verandah some time, exposed to the curiosity and to the jeers of the crowds of *chaprassis*, policemen, petition-writers, suitors, &c., some of whom occasionally refer unkindly to unwonted food as being ordinarily supplied to coolies in the colonies, or call them *mirchias,* which is supposed to embody a good deal that is dreadful. In the *cutcherry,* what with nervousness on being before a Magistrate and the difficulty of catching right away the accent of the foreigners who addresses him, the recruit is apt to lose his head and make absurd answers; a very possible result being that the Magistrate in his haste thinks all recruiters liars, and the one before him in particular a hardened villain, who has cruelly deceived a lot of ignorant people.

Further, if, when talking of the voyage, the words *kala pani* are used, the coolie is apt to lose all self-possession. *Kala pani* has long ago passed into the language as embodying the meaning of 'transportation' and so, when a coolie hears a Magistrate use the term, he thinks to himself: "what fault have I committed that I should be transported?" and promptly refuses to go. Nor will any one who knows our Courts assert that native Magistrates are, on an average, less rough and impatient in speech with nervous or stupid people brought up before them than are European Magistrates.

(3) The difficulties of emigration agents and recruiters, and the cost of recruiting to the colonies, are affected to a very serious degree by the different light in which the same Government order is read by different Magistrates.

For instance, Government in a circular enjoined that no recruit belonging to another district was to be registered, unless the Magistrate was satisfied that the recruit had not come to the place of registration solely on the inducement of the recruiter. Simple as this direction was, registration at some stations has been systematically refused of all coolies other than those belonging to the district itself.

In December, 1878, a resident of the Azamgarh district chose to turn his wife and two children out of doors. The woman wandered to Jaunpur, where her husband had a relative, but apparently failed to obtain help and joined the emigration depot.

Before the registering officer she stated that she was leaving the country because she had no one to support her, and eventually she sailed for Demerara. In the same batch was a coolie, who was rejected and sent back from Calcutta, and who must have known both the woman and her husband, as he managed to acquaint the husband of the wife having sailed. Then only, three months after the woman had been registered, did the husband petition Government. An enquiry was held, and no blame was attached to the recruiter; but Circular No. 88, dated July, 1879, was issued, enjoining registering officers, when registering married women, to ascertain in the best way available whether the husband be alive or dead, and, in the former case, whether the husband has any objection to his wife becoming an emigrant.

The majority of the women who come up for registration are either widows (often with families of small children) or married women who have misbehaved themselves, and have, in consequence, been turned out of house and home. A man who has turned his wife out of doors, if asked whether his wife might emigrate would probably say - no. In fact, when I was at Fyzabad, a woman was in the depot there, who had once been recruited, and had been sent back to her husband by the Magistrate, but who soon returned to the depot in a starving state. In a Lucknow village, I found a case where a married woman had emigrated because her husband had brought a strange woman into the house and had turned his wife out. The woman's own father told me the story. The only agency that the Magistrate can employ for such enquiries is the police. As the Resident, Hyderabad, on 19th August, 1881, in commenting on the new Emigration Bill, justly observed:

> "It is most undesirable to employ the police in domestic enquiries of this nature, which, if rigorously carried out, will involve the detention of all recruits for weeks in the local depots."

> "Thus the expense and risk attending the recruiter's operations will be much increased. Finally, if the section as drafted becomes law, 50 per cent of the recruits will be lost to the recruiters by rejection or desertion owing to long detention and police interference."

This I have found already proved. Registering officers in several districts have conceived it their duty under the circular above quoted to refuse to register all women unaccompanied by husbands until enquiries had been made through the police. As the replies to such enquiries, when sent to other districts, are seldom returned within three or four weeks, the women mostly fail to appear again, for the recruiter cannot always afford to keep them all that time. Sometimes the reply is received, 'not known at the address given,' and registration is then refused on the plea of the woman having given a false address; but my experience is, that the first impulse of a villager when enquiry is made from him about any one else is to deny all knowledge of that person until sure that any admission will not involve him in the trials and troubles of a Magisterial enquiry. Particularly is this likely to be the case where the interrogator is a police *sepoy*. At one station it was admitted that these police enquiries were instituted even in the case of women appearing with husbands, lest it should be a case of elopement. At another station all women unaccompanied by husbands were rejected without further enquiry, it being expected, I found, that even where the women's birth-place might be at the other end of India, she, or the recruiter, were expected to furnish 'evidence' that she was a widow.

68. The registration register should be prepared with great care to ensure that the names of the recruits, of their next of kin, and of their village, *pargana* and district are written distinctly and legibly. As a permanent record which may be required for reference in the case of an intestate estate 30 or 40 years after the date of registration, it should be on substantial paper and be strongly bound. The form might be altered with considerable advantage, and when once decided on, books with printed headings and of one uniform pattern should be issued to districts, and instructions of so plain and comprehensive a nature issued as to admit of no deviation. Further uniformity in practice might be secured by giving powers of inspection to one of those officers whose duties carry them all over the provinces during the cold weather.

69. Following strictly the reading of Act VII of 1871, only those coolies need be entered whom the Magistrate consents to register. It would be preferable to have all those presented for registration entered in the book, and the reasons for refusing registration, if any, fully entered in the column of remarks. This is already done in many districts.

The column of 'number' should be a serial one for all coolies presented, and should run for the calendar year. A 2nd column should be added giving a serial number for those passed of the batch, and commencing afresh with each batch. By the first of these two columns the Protector of Emigrants at Calcutta would be able to check the discrepancies complained of at page 9 of his report of 1879-80.

The name, father's name, sex, and caste to remain as at present, but the column of 'occupation' to be struck out. It is almost invariably filled up either with the word 'labourer,' or with the word 'cultivator.' As all engage as labourers their previous occupation is of little matter, and, in the Inland Emigration Act, this column is, I observe, omitted. Columns are required showing the children accompanying the emigrant classed as minors and infants and by sex, and a column for aged dependents, though it must be rare for one ever to go.

The column of next-of-kin requires an addition showing the relationship. Most of the additions suggested above I have found in various district registers.

The columns of terms of engagement and wages are, under the new Bill, to be left out of the register, and rightly so; at the most they need not have separate columns, but might be added to the heading.

It should be made obligatory on the Emigration Agency to forward to the registering officers, as soon as practicable, the name of ship, number on board that ship, and name of colony, of each coolie embarked. This to enable relatives to communicate. I have now numbers of applications from people anxious for the address of relatives who have emigrated, and I have had some difficulty in tracing them. It may seem superfluous to mention in the address the colony a second time, but it has happened that coolies have embarked for colonies other than the one for which they were first registered.

To enable the colonial authorities to refer back with greater ease and certainty of identification, questions regarding estates, reports of death, &c., I would strongly recommend the adoption of the following plan. Say that a coolie was registered at Lucknow for Trinidad in 1881, and that his serial number for the year was 500, then Lucknow 500/1881 or Lucknow/Trinidad, 500/1881 alone, if added to his name and father's name, would trace him more easily than at present appears to be possible, when half the difficulty of discovering the heirs to estates is owing to the extraordinary transformation often effected in a coolie's name after passing through two or three different hands. I would enter this identifying link on his contract, and insist on its being maintained in whatever lists or registers he may afterwards appear, forming as it were part and parcel of his name. I have by me now a list of remittances from coolies to friends in Oudh in which the Agent for Demerara has failed to trace the payee through Deputy Commissioners. The first remittance on the list was sent two years ago, and the village has evidently got muddled by some one, as 1 found the man's name and description in the Lucknow register, but with quite another village, and found his relatives easily enough. In the second case (remittance a year old) I recognised in 'Picconlie' a village called Paikoli, and found the man wanted in two days. A few weeks ago I recovered for a man in *pargana* Bijnor, Lucknow district, a remittance that came months ago and was supposed to be for a man in district Bijnor. I speak then from assured experience.

70. If registration is still to be carried on by the Magistrates, as at present, it would be a great improvement if it could be done on certain fixed days of the week, and anywhere but at the *cutcherry*. The municipal office, which the Magistrate has to visit pretty frequently in the early morning, is a place that suggests itself as convenient, and wherever Cantonment Magistrates exist, I would suggest their being invested with power to register, as not having so much case work as the district officers. In their case, of course, registration would have to be carried on at the cantonment *cutcherry*; but the crowd is there far smaller than at a district *cutcherry*.

71. Various plans in substitution of the present system have been proposed.

(a) That a special officer should be employed, who should travel from station to station and register coolies, a plan to my mind quite impracticable, unless it be intended to have registering offices only at a few places along the line of railway to which coolies from outlying districts would have to be brought. In this latter case, why register at all up-country? To secure an officer of sufficient standing for the responsibility involved high pay would have to be given. He could never afford to be ill, and would require rest sometimes, for such constant travelling would be excessively wearisome; and finally he would have far too little actual work to do to suit a conscientious man.

(b) Another proposal (my own) to employ treasury officers would not, I fear, work smoothly, as most of the treasury officers are natives, and my enquiries have convinced me that strong prejudices, or inability to use a wide discretion in carrying out orders on the part of native officers, render it necessary to place registration in the hands of European officers only. In letter No. 218, dated 24th December, 1879, from Government of India, to Government, North-Western Provinces, what I have stated above has been virtually admitted.

(c) The best proposal, in my humble judgment, is that of Mr. Ward, Collector of Jaunpur, who suggests that registration should be effected by the Civil Surgeon at the time of making the medical examination, which, under the new Bill, it is proposed to make compulsory. I have not as yet found any reasonable objection to this plan. Most district officers are distinctly in favour of it. At present, under a private arrangement with the Agencies, 6 *annas* per head is received as a fee for the medical examination. I would suggest its increase to 8 *annas* on the Civil Surgeon undertaking both duties, and would allow to his English clerk for keeping the register 2 *annas* per head, as is at present allowed in several districts of the North-Western Provinces.

The registration would be carried on on fixed days of the week either at the dispensary, the civil hospital, or at the Civil Surgeon's private residence where, I believe, the medical examination is now usually held.

This would enable a system to be introduced up-country of bringing up the coolie within 24 or 48 hours of his enlistment for examination as to whether he fully understands his mind about emigrating, so saving not only considerable expense to the Agencies, but also clearing the field in a great measure of the disputes which at present arise as to what has happened to the coolie while in depot awaiting registration.

72. Under this system it seems probable that an immense amount of time, trouble, and friction would be saved, and I think it only reasonable to expect that the small extra expense of the fee would be covered by the readier flow of recruits. To the Civil Surgeon also might be made over the duty of occasionally inspecting the local depot. There does not seem to me to be any choice beyond leaving registration with Magistrates as now, only confining it to Europeans, and placing it in the hands of Civil Surgeons, as recommended.

73. Sir Ashley Eden wrote from Burmah in 1871, that "there should be no possibility of crimping if only the Magistrate will conscientiously and scrupulously examine the intending emigrants instead of passing them as a mere matter of form. He believes that the whole of the evils of the system are to be traced to carelessness and indifference on the part of the Magistrate."

The above is a strong opinion from [a] strong man. It is my most humble opinion that the enquiry of the Magistrate, if conducted in a temperate and conscientious manner, is quite sufficient to cure deception; and that, so long as the medical officer passes the emigrant as being of sufficient age, he or she should be allowed to go without further enquiry, should they so wish, despite the objections of relatives. It would be sufficient to meet the cases of single women without children, to rule that such women should not be removed from the local depot under a week or ten days from entry therein, which should be time enough to admit of any husband in search of a runaway wife finding and claiming her; but if, as no doubt often happens, the woman has been turned out of home, she should be allowed to emigrate if she prefers to do so, unless the husband furnishes security, for her good treatment.

VI. Whether the system of recruiting females needs reform

74. This question I will take to include another which came up at the Calcutta Emigration Meeting, viz., whether the system of requiring a certain proportion of women to men in each shipment should not be relaxed so as to admit of the surplus of one season counting for another; and further, whether licenses should be granted to female recruiters.

75. I think that the system does need very great reform

(1) As to the local depots. In every local depot arrangements should be made (as has been already suggested) for the complete separation of single women and married people from single men, and a woman should be in charge of that part of the depot. In some of the depots I have visited, men and women were crowded together in a small space with one latrine common to all, and no attempt at separation either by day or night, rendering common decency and modesty impossible. All female relatives or connections of the depot establishment should be strictly excluded unless residing under special permission. It should then be difficult for such cases to occur as have hitherto frequently cropped up, of women complaining on arrival at Calcutta that they had been living with the recruiter as his mistress, and had got themselves registered at the recruiter's request in order to obtain a free passage to Calcutta.

(2) The system of enquiry through the police has been alluded to as having a most detrimental effect on the females. If my proposition, that the detention of all single women in depot of a week or 10 days, so as to admit of their being reclaimed if required by relatives, in lieu of police enquiries, does not find favour, then I would substitute enquiry through *kanungos* and *patwaris* for that through the police. Where women have small children with them they are in most cases widows, and a little quiet cross-questioning should always enable the registering officer to ascertain under what circumstances the woman has resolved to emigrate, and detention need only be ordered in suspicious cases.

(3) Many of the women arrive at the depot in a state bordering on nudity. In the opinion of experienced recruiters the grant of a *dhoti* (cost under one *rupee*) would greatly popularise recruiting, and would go far towards lowering the excess difference which at present has to be paid as commission for a woman.

(4) As regards recruiting, I started with a strong feeling against the employment of female recruiters, but have seen reason to change my opinions to some extent. Of those with whom I have spoken on the subject, the recruiters have been the foremost opponents of the idea, which I take to be a proof that the scheme would succeed. It is already carried on to some extent illegally by female relatives or friends of recruiters or *chaprassis,* and the necessity of employing women stands to reason, as it is only women at their last resource who would bargain with strange men. The chief difficulty would be to obtain women of sufficient rectitude, energy, and acuteness to hold their own amongst the trials incident to a recruiter's career. The class, however, can no doubt be found just as native women are found who can efficiently act as ticket-collectors and *zenana* carriage doorkeepers on the Oudh and Rohilkhand Railway. It might be advisable to make women-recruiters give some security for good behaviour, and only permit them at first to recruit at a few selected stations. Women who have already been to the colonies, and who, besides acquiring habits of independence, can speak from personal knowledge of colonial advantages, would probably succeed best. The colonies might help by offering premiums to any woman who might re-emigrate and bring

other women with them. That police enquiries check more than anything else the recruiting of women the study of district registers has quite satisfied me.

76. From all that I have read on the subject, and from information gained in conversation with an officer who has within the last few years visited nearly all the West India Islands as well as British Guiana, and from what the returned emigrants have told me, I should be more inclined to insist on raising the present limit of 40 per cent of women to one of 50 per cent rather than to lower it; still, I think there is much to recommend itself in the proposal that the surplus women of one season might count towards the next season: this to effect future shipments only and not to have retrospective effect. We have it in evidence from the Emigration Agents that, to enable a ship to start, they are occasionally compelled to enlist in the slums of Calcutta the very worst of characters. The effect of sending such creatures is simply to intensify the evils complained of. Nearly every returned emigrant, after praising everything he can think of in and about the colonies, winds up by saying "but, sahib, there is one bad thing, and that is the women." On vantage ground from the fewness of their numbers, they go from one to the other as fancy or cupidity dictates, and cause constant quarrels and jealousies. Admittedly, the worse the character of the women sent, the greater this evil. The hard-and-fast rule of refusing to allow vessels to proceed without the full proportion of women places it within the power of the sub-agents up-country to put pressure on the agents to raise the rates for women. The plan of allowing the surplus women of one season to count towards the next might well have a trial for, say, five years.

A singular illustration of the effect on fancy produced by this scarcity of females was given me by a returned emigrant, remarking, with reference to the climate, that the women seemed to grow younger after arrival and never looked old.

I may mention here that fear of the medical examination has in all probability some effect in preventing females from enlisting, and that it would be advisable for the examination to be conducted, as far as possible, by the *dhai* usually attached, I believe, to the civil hospital.

76a. The following extract from letter No. 76, dated 22nd March, 1882, from the Lieutenant-Governor, British Guiana, to the Government of India, may be appropriately quoted here:

76b. "But there is one blot connected with the immigration system which should be removed - a blot which the colonies are most earnest in their desire to remove, and one which, with the cordial aid and co-operation of the Government of India, may, it is to be hoped, be removed at some not very distant day. I allude to the disproportion of the sexes. The Indian population will not mix with the negro population, and a community in which the males are as 2 to 1 to the females must ever be a source of anxiety to the governing power, and can never be expected, as a whole, to develop a high order of morality. The colonies by themselves are powerless in this matter. It is to the Indian Government alone that they can look for help. Under existing laws and restrictions, it is with the utmost difficulty that the minimum proportion of females can now be obtained as emigrants, and to increase that proportion would but prevent emigration altogether, But I understand that if certain existing laws and restrictions were removed, and the individual rights as human beings of women were more distinctly recognised and protected, the number of females ready and anxious to emigrate might be greatly augmented. It is neither within the scope of this despatch nor within my province to suggest in what manner existing obstructions to the emigration of females might be modified. What we would earnestly desire is that the Government of India should, with its better knowledge and better judgment, be induced to consider this important question, as not only affecting the interests of the coolie-importing colonies, but also as very deeply affecting the interests of those natives of India who desire to seek elsewhere a livelihood that they cannot secure in their own country."

VII. Whether there is any hope of inducing families to emigrate

77. Yes, I think there is, through the agency of old emigrants.

I frequently converse upon this point with intending emigrants, a large proportion of whom leave families behind, and am smilingly assured that it is out of the question to expect respectable men, however ready themselves to venture on the unknown, to expose their wives to they know not what sort of risks. It is the custom of the country that, when a man goes abroad to seek a livelihood, his wife and children are supported by his or her relatives until he returns.

Failure of duty in this respect is visited with expulsion from caste by the rest of the community, influenced by the natural law of self-preservation. Every year, all over the country, sees the surplus male population of the villages issue forth to seek service, leaving families at home whom they may not see for years.

If the amounts remitted to their families by these absentees through post-office orders and *hundis* could be ascertained, the figures would be startling in their magnitude.

78. I am confident that if the emigrants could only be certain of the money reaching their families, and could remit at a reasonable rate, the number of remittances would increase enormously, and remittances would be made to enable families to follow their relatives. Four such remittances were made last year to the Fyzabad district.

The object of the remittance when the family proceeds at the expense of the colonies is, probably, to pay off debts for which otherwise the family might be detained.

It only requires energy and common sense to be applied to revising the present system of correspondence and remittance between emigrants and their families to produce, in my humble opinion, a most favourable effect on emigration. During my district tour I could only hear of one man who had ever received a remittance. I have another case in hand already alluded to in para. 69, where I have just succeeded in realising for an emigrant's family a remittance which was sent to them ten months ago.

79. Judging from the registers, families amongst the lower castes emigrate pretty freely during years of scarcity, but ordinarily it is amongst those re-emigrating, and the people whom they induce to accompany them, that families predominate.

80. Formerly it was the custom for either Mauritius or Reunion to make an advance of wages to emigrants. Such an advance would much promote the emigration of families in helping them to pay off

the creditors who might otherwise bar the way, but there would be complicated accounts and perhaps dishonest trading on these advances.

81a. Section 35 of the new Emigration Bill in enabling parents to contract for their children will doubtless prove a powerful stimulus to the emigration of families.

81b. The medical examination of females should be relaxed on certain points when women accompany their husbands as likely otherwise to have a deterring effect, and the absence hitherto of arrangements in the depot for insuring ordinary decency may possibly have some effect in deterring men from taking their wives with them.

VIII. What, if any, are the objections of natives to emigrate and if they can be overcome?

82. The objections of the natives to emigrate may be thus stated:

(1) A dread of interference with caste
(2) A dread of forcible conversion to Christianity
(3) A dread of the unknown, common to all ignorant and untraveled people
(4) A strong suspicion that the whole business is a fraud, a suspicion very naturally arising from the paucity of news received from those who have gone away, and from the small percentage who ever return.

83. Objections (1) and (2) can only be met by increased care being taken to guard against interference with either caste or religion. Caste has its disadvantages, but, in its sleepless vigil over the moralities, it saves us here in India a vast expenditure which would otherwise have to be incurred for increased police, and so too with religions. Better, surely, for the coolies their ancient beliefs than none at all; and although there may be no overt acts in the direction of forcible conversion, they may well come to look in time at any discouragement of their forms of worship as being prompted by religious hate.

84. Objections (3) and (4) can no doubt be overcome like all other groundless fears by ocular or by oral demonstration. Ocularly, by the return of emigrants to their homes, and orally, by every effort being put forward to promote correspondence.

85. In the Emigration Report for British Guiana for the year 1881, the number of letters despatched by emigrants during 1880 is given as 511, and this for a resident Indian population of from 80,000 to 90,000. To popularise emigration, correspondence should be forced up to 20,000 of either letters or post-cards per annum. The report goes on to say, "Under a well-organised system, this correspondence would become more general amongst the emigrants, and, with that object in view, a scheme has been prepared which with such modifications as may be deemed necessary, will, I trust, be brought here long into operation."

I cannot discover that, since the above was written, any further steps have been taken in the matter.

86. It is for the planters, who ask for more and for better men, to bestir themselves in this matter by making arrangements to ensure that every coolie under indenture, who possesses friends in Hindustan, shall send a letter or post-card at least once a year, and further encourage them by all the persuasion in their power to remit money.

87. The postage rates from India to the various colonies for letters[2] and post-cards are simply prohibitory in some cases to the relatives here, and one may fairly think that the large correspondence, which lower rates for coolie emigrants might bring about, would pay better than the present high rates and small number of letters. The foreign-residing coolie population is about 750,000. A postal delivery in India of 100,000 letters per annum should be attainable.

88. Remittances to India from Demerara (exclusive of the sums brought back by returning coolies) amounted in 1873 to only Rs. 51. Not much, it will be allowed, for over 80,000 people to send to their relatives out of the splendid wages which we know so many of them get. This sum has risen to Rs. 2,217-7-1 in 1878.

89. I have already alluded to the popular belief that emigrants are sent to populate desert countries, and am sure that a large section of the native public continue to disbelieve in the promise of a free return passage.

Possibly those who hold to these opinions look upon the comparatively small proportion who come within their kin that have hitherto returned, as so many lucky men who have escaped.

This belief must have grown out of the fact that recruits are engaged for all British colonies for a term of five years, and yet, only get a free return passage after ten years; while for the French colonies the engagement is also for five years, with, however, a free passage after five years.

Between the two a general idea has arisen that the coolie ought to return after five years, and that if he does not then return he may be given up. Seeing that so small a proportion do re-appear, so far, after even ten years, a man who has emigrated is in most districts given up as lost. That this feeling should exist to any degree is clearly as detrimental to emigration as any thing could well be.

90. The returned emigrant with 18 years' experience of Demerara, to whom I have once before alluded, tells me that since drinking has been put down among the coolies in that colony, there has been a marked increase in self-respect and morality, and a more general desire to revisit home than formerly.

91. The colonial authorities, by grants of land and bounties, tempt time-expired men to stay. In my humble opinion it would be a wiser policy if, for a few years to come, another plan were given a trial, and that is to encourage all good men entitled to a free passage to return to their homes, undertaking with such as might be worth retaining to give them on re-emigrating such advantages in the way of curtailment of indenture and grants of land as the colony could afford. The grant or terms might be proportionately increased for every coolie whom the returning emigrant might succeed in inducing to accompany him. Under such a system, continued for say ten years, a more popular knowledge of emigration would spread through the recruiting field, and in this idea I am supported by the practical opinion of the emigrant I have above referred to. Anthony Trollope wrote: "It is natural enough

that men should hesitate to trust themselves to a future of which they know nothing. It required that some few should come out and prosper and return with signs of prosperity."

92. Through a returned French emigrant I am informed that drinking and gambling prevails amongst the coolies resident in the French colonies to a deplorable extent, and that the reason for so few returning from Guadeloupe and Martinique when their five years' term expires, is due to cash bounties being offered in lieu of passage, which bounties are speedily gambled away. My information may be wrong, but I fail from the correspondence to discover that Government has any better. Coolies do certainly not return from the French colonies in such numbers as might fairly be expected.

93. Emigration would further acquire more popularity if greater pains were taken to ensure the estates of deceased persons reaching the next of kin. It has been stated as a fact worthy of notice that (in British Guiana) of all the wills or documents of a testamentary nature made by coolies up to 1877 *in not one of them has any bequest or legacy been made to any relative or friend in India.* The same letter in another paragraph says: "Few single men die possessed of much property, and they seldom die intestate. Generally a single man associates himself with another, they live together in the same room, their property is common, and when one of them dies the other being in possession succeeds to it." Again, in para. 11: "A manager of an estate is bound to report to me (the Administrator-General) the death of all coolies who die on the estate under his charge, whether possessed of property or not; but as a rule the deaths of those only *who die possessed of property* are reported to me.*"*

Surely this state of things is not satisfactory to any friend of the coolie. We have, on the one hand, colonial official assurances that few single men die possessed of much property, that a bequest to friends and relatives in India is never made, and that whether an estate manager reports the death of a coolie or not is a matter for his own conscience.

On the other hand, we have shiploads of returned emigrants each year, 50 per cent of whom are single men bringing large sums of money and other valuable property, a fact, very properly much advertised.

We have it in evidence that the yearly remittances to friends in India are on the increase, and there is every reason to believe that if a remittance could be made as easily and safely as it can be in India through the post-office, that these remittances would expand enormously, and we know that many of these so-called single men dying in the colonies have relatives and families in India.

The coolie's behaviour regarding his colonial estate carries to my mind the conviction that the coolie has lost all confidence and trust in the procedure formulated for conveying estates, testate or intestate, to friends and relatives in India. It were better for the colonies than this that if, when being registered, the coolie says he has no heir, he were urged to nominate as his heir some one or other of his village acquaintances or even the *lambardar*. A few hundreds of *rupees* falling in to *lambardars* in this way would put a smile or two on the aspect of emigration.

94. The subject is one which the Indian Government is bound to enquire into very strictly for the sake of the unfortunate and helpless women and children in this country, and which the Colonial Government will find to their own benefit to set on a just and liberal footing. The present machinery is too cumbrous, lists of names occasionally appear in Gazettes which never reach the people, and in which the names of persons and places have, under the system of transliteration in vogue in the colonies, become completely disguised. A few examples taken out of Government of India Proceedings are Fokheer Kham (for Fakir Khan) Bedessy (for Badesi) Ram Logone (for Ram Lagan) and Anjoow for I cannot say what. If the system of register numbers for each coolie were adopted, the original register could be referred to.

95. Here I must say that since interviewing the families of emigrants at their homes the inhumanity of not ensuring that information of an emigrant's death should if possible, be communicated to his family or relatives, has revealed itself to me in a manner which no amount of 'interest in emigration' would otherwise have done. I found in village after village women with children who had waited faithfully for news, some as long as 18 years, others, not so faithful, who had married again. Some provision should be taken in the new Bill for communicating the death of an emigrant to his friends.

Government can certainly do more in many ways to encourage emigration. An order exists that copies of the terms offered by each colony shall be hung up at every *tahsil*. These notices may have been hung up at all *tahsils* when the original order came out; but, it being no one's business to see that they are maintained, scarcely one *tahsil* will be found with them now. These terms should be painted or pasted on to boards, and posted at the *thanahs* and *tahsils* of such districts as recruiting may be active in.

The colonies publish papers in English and Vernacular setting forth in full the various advantages of each colony. Every *tahsildar* and Inspector of police should be furnished with a copy of such papers, and this 'statement of advantages' should be read in full to the coolies at the time of registration by the registration clerk, a practice which I found had under one officer been carried out.

96. I have already remarked that the idea of any one commanding implicit obedience simply because he happens to be a Government servant is, I believe, highly exaggerated. The exact amount of power wielded by each officer is duly appraised. Government servants of the army, for instance, are powerless practically to obtain supplies unless backed up by the civil authorities of the district, and the Collector of one district who ventures into another district when on tour without a *parwanah* finds himself in hostile country.

97. A singular illustration of the idea that a Government servant commands universal submission is exemplified in the proposal to be found in the new Emigration Bill, that recruiters shall no longer wear badges 'lest they should be mistaken for Government servants', when, as a matter of fact, not only do regimental messes and institutions, clubs, libraries, merchants, European and native, and every petty contractor mount all their *chaprassis* with badges, but in Oudh it is quite common for the *taluqdars* to do so, and no inconvenience has hitherto been found to arise from the practice.

98. What the mass of the population really exercise their powers of observation in, is to notice the exact degree of favour or countenance received by each Department working with the sanction of the State, and to accord to it an equivalent amount of respect, and no more.

From the time that Government insists on the Magistracy giving emigration all the help they legitimately can, and Magistrates show the people and particularly the police, that they intend so to do, emigration will become more popular.

IX. Whether coolie emigration is more popular in some districts than in others and if so, why?

99. This question has to some extent been already answered.

So far as emigration can be said to be more popular in one district than another, it is so

(1) in those districts where are to be found the greatest number of return emigrants.
(2) where district and police officers give emigration their support and sympathy.

100. Figures show that at least one-third of the people recruited in any one district are pauper wanderers from other districts, while another section are likewise outsiders with reasons of their own for quitting home for a time. This year and next year a good number of emigrants are expected to return to the eastern districts of Oudh, and the recruiters anticipate as a result a greater flow of emigration from thence.

Appendix V shows distribution by residence of the emigrants from the North-Western Provinces and Oudh for 1881-82 and the proportionate amount of emigrants from each district. I have been surprised by the number of Afghans and Peshawar hill men in the depots of late, and the finest batch of men I have yet seen was one of 30 comprising the first men ever recruited so high up-country as Amritsur. Many of these men had been through the war in the Land Transport Corps, some through the Abyssinian war, and one to Malta. The Panjab is a field that might be worked with a depot at Karachi for Natal or for Queensland with advantage to the land, as recruiters report that the number of men seeking work is excessive. These Amritsur men, I may note, were extremely anxious to know whether they could remit freely to their families from Fiji, to which colony they were proceeding.

X. Whether emigration to some colonies is more popular than to others, or whether coolies generally exhibit when enlisting an intelligent preference for one colony over another

101. Amongst returned emigrants there seem to be some popular notions on the subject. Trinidad (Chini Tat) has the preference, then Demerara (Damra or Demeraila). All speak well of Jamaica. Little is known yet of either Fiji or Natal. Mauritius (More-righteous and Mirch) is admitted to have advantages in the shortness of the journey, the cheapness of the return passage, and (for the lazy) in the payments of monthly wages in the place of a daily task, or rather piecework: but industrious people prefer the latter. Rightly or wrongly, Mauritius has acquired a doubtful reputation in some of the lower districts, and at Gorakhpur I was told by a recruiter that coolies would sometimes say that they were ready to go to any colony but Mauritius. We know from the latest report that this feeling is most unjust to Mauritius of the present day, and any discredit attaching to it must be a reflection of the old days of 'vagrant hunts,' or, of its French neighbour Bourbon (Birboon).

Over the French colonies heads are shaken. French masters are credited with beating their coolies, and with indifference to the coolie's morality in the direction of drinking and gambling. No one appears ever to have met or heard of any coolie who had been to Cayenne. Of Surinam, it is said that the coolies are not so well housed and looked after as they are in Demerara, and that they do not earn so much money, but that the Dutch are kind masters. Such little as has been heard of Natal is good.

102. I confess that I do not like to see these opinions confined to old emigrants. It is a matter for deep regret that the flow of our people towards any particular colony does not follow as a consequence of the popularity of a colony so much as of the activity of its agents. A man, seeing a neighbour return from Trinidad with a small fortune, sets off to emigrate but happens to meet an Agent of Bourbon or Martinique. To the coolie it is all *Tapu* till he gets there, but his chances are distinctly not the same in every case. The voyage to Fiji is 18 weeks, and to Jamaica 20 weeks. In the coolie's imagination you go past Fiji to Jamaica, and it is as well to save time, so why not stop at Fiji? The ordinary recruiter is no wiser.

103. Nor can any one like to see the existence of a practice amongst sub-agents of transferring coolies from one to another, like cattle, for a consideration, nominally on payment of expenses, but which, no doubt, includes some share of the prospective profit. For instance, I found a case upcountry occurring only last month, where a batch of men had been recruited for Fiji but not registered. A sub-agent of the Mauritius arrived accompanied by a recruiter, exhibited the license of the latter for countersignature, and, having arranged for the transfer of the Fiji men, registered them as recruited for Mauritius. No doubt the coolies were duly informed and duly consented; but most people would prefer to see the coolie less passive in the transaction. Every season it happens in the Calcutta depots that some recruits arrive too late for the last ship of some particular colony, and it becomes necessary to give them choice of discharge or of proceeding to some other colony, but there everything is done under the Protector's sanction.

104. More direct instruction of the people as to the advantages tendered them by different colonies is, I submit, called for, and towards the efficient communication of such instruction more information regarding the colonies, particularly the foreign ones, than we now possess, is required.

XI. In the transport of the coolies from the local depots to Calcutta, can any improvements be suggested?

105. In each compartment of an ordinary 3rd class carriage there are 10 seats, which gives the occupants bare sitting room. In short distance journeys this, of course, does not matter, but when it comes to the longer journeys, from Benares and higher up-country, the inconvenience is serious. Unless the recruiter, or *chaprassi* in charge, can keep his batch continually together, he runs great risk of losing some of them, particularly those who may be unaccustomed to long railway journey. When outsiders get mixed up with the coolies, it sometimes happens that they endeavour to frighten the latter with alarming tales. So also when a train stops for any length of time, it is much complained of that the railway police and Railway Company's servants, frequenting the platforms, amuse themselves by teasing the coolies. Within the last three or four months a railway servant in this

way so excited a batch of coolies, when halted at a small station, that many left the train and refused to proceed.

106. Over 40,000 coolies have passed down to Calcutta from Ghazipur and stations above within the last four years, and with emigration open to Queensland and South Australia, these numbers may be expected to increase. Then we have an unknown number proceeding every year to Assam, and Cachar. In view of this custom, I think that the Railway Companies might fairly grant the concession of putting only eight emigrants in one compartment, and reserving such compartments strictly throughout the journey to Calcutta, particularly when it is remembered that ordinary travellers cram the carriages with various belongings, while emigrants carry no baggage.

107. Better still, if a class of carriages were built for the special accommodation of coolies with double or treble rows, of benches lengthways, the lower one close to the floor, there being no baggage, and with latrine accommodation at the end of the carriage.

108. Station-masters should be instructed to give recruiters help when annoyed by the jeers of people connected or unconnected with the railway.

XII. Whether any alterations in the present system of levying fees for registration and for licenses seems desirable?

109. Acknowledging the difficulties attendant on a system in which every sub-agent and recruiter would be paid by salary in the place of contract, I still think that every effort should be made to eliminate from the present contract system all payments which, as being certain and ascertained sums, should be paid direct by Emigration Agents, and not be included in the contract, such as the hire of depots, recruiters' license fees, railway fares, and registration fees.

110. From some remarks in the emigration correspondence, it seems to be the idea in some quarters that the fee of Re. 1-8-0 paid by the recruiter on the registration of each recruit is a prerequisite of the Magistrates, whereas it is paid into the Treasury, and trickling down

through various channels to Calcutta goes there to form an Emigration Fund under the Local Government from which the Protector and Medical Inspector of Emigrants, together with their establishments, are paid. So long as those expenses are covered, it seems immaterial what fee or how large a fee is paid within, of course, reasonable limits.

111. The object aimed at could be attained with more ease and certainty and in a more economical way by the sum required being ascertained and the Colonial Agents paying such proportionate fee on each coolie actually embarked during the year as would cover the amount required. A fixed monthly payment based on the operations of the preceding year might be fixed subject to adjustment at the end of the year.

112. Such a system would simplify the work of a large number of Government officers and would at the same time very much simplify the work and accounts of sub-agents and recruiters. The fee can scarcely be called a check on the recruiter who is otherwise checked by the cost of feeding the coolie and of paying his railway fare. The recruiter would still have to pay the fee of one or two *annas* per head to the English clerk for writing up the forms and register.

113. As for licenses, since the amount paid for them would go towards the Emigration Fund, it would not really matter under this system whether they were paid for at all or what particular sum was fixed. I am of opinion that it would better answer the purpose aimed at to abolish fees and in their place to require that each sub-agent and recruiter furnish security for good conduct (as proposed by Mr. Ward, Collector of Jaunpur) to a reasonable amount, the security to be a householder, and any fine up to the amount of the bond to be realisable from the security in the manner provided in the case of defaulting Government servants.

114. Depot servants should also take out licenses, but in their case it might be difficult to find security, and besides the sub-agents or recruiters would be mainly responsible for any misconduct of a depot servant, as such.

XIII. Whether there are any points in the procedure with reference to returned emigrants calling for notice?

115. An emigrant should be as carefully protected back to his home as he was protected away from it. No more money should be paid to the returned emigrant, on arrival in Calcutta, out of his savings, than he may absolutely require; the balance should be remitted for him to the treasury of the district to which he proposes returning and the various ways by which he may safely invest his money with Government until he wishes to draw it for private uses, such as the Postal Savings Banks, Stock Notes, &c., should be carefully explained.

As it is, many of the men are, I believe, paid off large sums in Calcutta immediately on disembarkation, only to get fleeced and robbed by swindlers, who lie in wait for them, before ever they can get away from Calcutta itself. It should rather be the rule that a man should not be paid off in Calcutta unless he urgently desires money there.

116. A return should be sent to the Collector of each district to which emigrants may be returning, giving simply name, caste, village and *pargana,* and in the Collectorate these names and particulars should be recorded in a register. If this were done Collectors who took an interest in the matter might when on tour find out from some of these men a good deal of information which would be of use to Government, perhaps, when emigration questions cropped up. It would be a potent means towards making emigration more popular, as the people generally would soon copy the Collector's example in making enquiries, and so learn for themselves.

117. I hardly think that Colonial Planters can be aware of the inordinate value attached by Asiatics to 'chits' or testimonials. If they were, they would be careful to give every man of good conduct, on leaving, a testimonial as to character. Better still, if the Colonial Authorities would give to the well-conducted certificates of good conduct when leaving, and the more highly emblazoned the better. Such testimonials would be flourished by the emigrant on return to the envy of his village neighbours, who, with reference to any outward signs, of wealth, might remark that 'perhaps he stole it' (vide instance in my diary), but would look on the 'chit' or certificate with real respect. A returned emigrant

exhibited to me the other day, with a face full of honest pride, a receipt in English for the price of a cow which he had bought from some planter for 40 dollars.

XIV. Under what arrangements is the purely clerical work of registration conducted, and does any alteration seem call for?

118. Not only has the registration clerk a good deal to do, but it is of great importance that what he does should be done really well. Illegibility in writing and carelessness or ignorance in the transliteration of names gives rise sometimes to months of delay and multifold correspondence when a remittance has to be paid to a coolie's friends, or enquiries have to be made about next of kin.

119. It stands to reason that the work is likely to be more speedily and effectively performed, and the recruiter subjected to less delay at *cutcherry* when the clerk receives remuneration, than when the case is otherwise. In several stations where emigration was working smoothly, I found the clerks in charge taking a most intelligent interest in the subject, and able to indicate for some time back entries in the register worthy of note.

120. No provision for the payment for this work was made in any of the Emigration Acts, but in letter No. 2731, dated 13th October, 1866, the Government of India gave permission to the Government, North-Western Provinces to authorise, when circumstances seemed to require it, the payment to a writer employed in the registration of emigrants of an allowance of two *annas* per head.

Accordingly, for a few stations only in the North-Western Provinces, the payment was sanctioned, while in Oudh in 1873 a payment of one *anna* per head was sanctioned for Lucknow and Fyzabad only.

121. Consequently, when on tour I found the remuneration for the same labour in three adjoining districts to be thus: Bara Banki, nil; Fyzabad, one *anna* per head: Basti, two *annas* per head. Naturally these distinctions without a difference formed a grievance with some of the clerks, and had in some few districts led to the recruiters being forced to get written out in the *bazaars,* per chance by some illiterate

school boy who might be playing truant, the lists which it is I maintain so important to have written correctly. The clerks in Oudh were doing their work on one *anna* just as well as those who were elsewhere getting two *annas,* but in view of the register proposed being somewhat more elaborate than the one hitherto maintained, I would beg to recommend that the registration clerks at all stations in the United Provinces should alike receive two *annas* per head. The work must be given, it may be observed, to some clerk as extra work. Taking the registration of the last four years, Benares heads the list with a total of 5,064 coolies for that period. At two *annas* per head this would give the clerk Rs. 13-3-0 per mensem, for which sum it would be impossible to secure the exclusive services of a really competent English writer.

XV. Complaints have lately been made of the occurrence amongst newly-arrived coolies in Demerara of cases of epilepsy and weak intellect, and of the number of new arrivals who have to be sent to hospital within a short time after landing. How far does this seem to be due to faulty arrangements in up-country recruiting?

122. Besides the coolies recruited up-country, there are a certain number recruited in Calcutta itself between whom and embarkation considerably less time elapses than in the case of the up-country men. It would have been better I think, to refer back the numbers of the coolies alluded to as weak in intellect and epileptic, so that the period passed by them in depot might be ascertained, and likewise the stations at which they were medically examined. As the up-country recruiter has to bear the entire cost of any recruit rejected in Calcutta including railway fare to Calcutta and back, food, registration fee, &c., it seems unlikely on the face of it that the recruiters would willingly send unsound recruits. A column might be added to the register giving the descriptive marks of the recruit: but I hardly think the gain would be worth the very great additional trouble involved. Such a column existed in the early registers in one of which I found it filled up for months of unvarying monotony with the words 'of a black colour.'

123. With reference to the greater prevalence of disease amongst new arrivals I may note, for what it may be worth, what a returned emigrant told me - namely, that amongst the coolies it was rumoured that in the

early days of emigration to Demerara no coolie was set to work for some days after landing; whereas now, if to all appearance fit for work, he is set to work immediately, and, as a consequence, that more men now fall sick in the early days of their residence than was formerly the case. This information was volunteered to me before I had an opportunity of seeing the medical report on British Guiana for 1880. It seems to stand to reason that some rest should be given to allow of the digestive organs accommodating themselves to the change from ship life and food to the conditions of shore life.

XVI. Whether daily payments in cash might not be substituted for rations in the up-country depots when the coolies have to be detained for long periods

124. Since commencing this report, I have had some experience in the Lucknow depots of the recruiting, which commences from 1st June or so for Demerara and Trinidad. The ships do not sail from Calcutta until July. Meanwhile the coolies accumulate to overflowing in the up-country depots. Apart from the objection of over-crowding, the coolies are, I find, apt to grow suspicious at the long detention, and to consider that they are losing time in which they might otherwise be earning money over and above the cost of their food. No doubt the cost of feeding them up-country is less than in Calcutta, but it seems only fair that, if a man is detained in depots over a certain time, he should receive some small wage in cash representing the sum put aside by an ordinary day labourer over and above the cost of his own food for the support of those dependent on him, or else give him cash instead of rations, as is done in the Trinidad depot at Calcutta.

I think there would then be less loss from desertions than there is now. I have found, too, the existence of a report which has evidently been lately spread by malicious people, that coolies never receive wages in the colonies, but only food, and at my last visit to a depot I was anxiously interrogated on this point. It so happened that I had just received some remittances which I had recovered for the relatives of certain emigrants. These remittances I paid over in the presence of the depots' coolies, and the effect was so good that I should recommend remittances being always, where possible, delivered to the payee in the presence of the coolies collected at the local depots.

A native gentleman calling on me lately mentioned quite casually the fact that he had recently heard that coolies were never paid any wages, and that if, as I assured him, they were paid as promised, then in his opinion, the Magistrates should at registration remove the coolies doubts on this score.

With the change contemplated in the new Bill, whereby coolies who desert after registration can be punished by the Magistrate, and with registration and the depots system so regulated as to admit of every coolie being registered at the most within three days of his entering a depot, I think it is a point for consideration with the Agents whether the coolie should not up-country be paid daily in cash, on the system pursued in the Trinidad depot at Calcutta, or partly in cash and partly in kind, instead of wholly in kind, as is usually done at present. It may be said that a sufficient number, or nearly so, are secured under present arrangements; but I submit that it is in quality that the present supply of recruits most needs improvement, and that every little step made towards gaining the confidence of the people is likely to aid in improving the average quality of the recruit supply.

XVII. General summary of the principal recommendations made

1. Sub-agents to be licensed specially as such, and, further, to be allowed to exercise all powers exercised by ordinary recruiters, to pay no license fee, but to furnish substantial security for good behaviour; to be remunerated partly by monthly salary and partly by commission, on the system at present pursued by the Trinidad Agency.

2. Recruiters to pay no license fee, but to furnish substantial security to a moderate amount for good conduct, to be relieved from paying the fee at registration, to wear badges as heretofore, and to be confined in their contracts to as few items of charge as possible. A license to be cancelled only on a judicial proceeding, and the judgment to be appealable to the Commissioner. Any augmentation of the penalties provided for offences by recruiters under Act VII of 1871 strongly deprecated, and the reduction of a recruiter from 1st to 2nd grade recommended as a punishment for minor offences. That provision be made in the new Bill making wilful obstruction and insult to a recruiter in respect to his calling punishable with a small fine; that provision be

made by detailed rules for the prompt and summary settlement of quarrels or disputes in the depot, previous to registration, between the recruiter and his recruits.

3. A register to be kept at each depot of all persons attached to it, and of all coolies entering the depot. No transfers to be allowed from one colony to another until sanction has been obtained from the Magistrate.

4. Every person, other than a sub-agent or a recruiter, employed at a depot to be licensed with a 2nd grade license. All unlicensed persons, other than coolies, to be rigidly excluded from depots. The employment of returned emigrants as recruiters and *chaprassis* suggested as practicable.

5. Separate accommodation under charge of a female servant to be provided in each depot for single women and married people.

6. Female recruiters to be given a trial experimentally within a limited area.

7. Blankets to be supplied to the coolies during the cold-weather months.

8. Depots to be inspected by and to be under the control of European Magistrates, Medical Officers, or District Superintendents of Police.

9. Registration to be conducted as at present, but by European Magistrates only, or preferably by Medical Officers simultaneously with the medical examination; the Medical Officer to receive a combined fee on the two duties of eight *annas* on each emigrant passed at the final medical examination in Calcutta. Registration to take place as soon as practicable after the entry of the coolie into depot.

10. Expenses of the Calcutta protective establishments to be realised by a proportionate fee on each coolie embarked.

11. Local registers to be kept by the Medical Officer's English clerk, who should receive for so doing two *annas* per head, no matter how few the number registered.

12. To preserve uniformity, registers to be inspected by some one inspecting officer for the province.

13. Copies of register to be sent monthly to the local Agricultural Department.

14. New form of register suggested particularly to include the emigrant's colonial address, and so adapted as to maintain for him a serial number in the original register. All persons presented for registration to be entered on the register.

15. A register of returned emigrants in short form to be maintained, and advice and help in the protection of their savings to be given them.

16. Information of death and desertion of emigrants to be reported to the registering officer, to be by him noted in the register and to be posted officially by card to the registered next-of-kin, if any.

17. Postage to be reduced to the lowest practicable rate, and correspondence by post-card or otherwise to be stimulated by judicious pressure.

18. Remittances likewise to be stimulated, and some system less complicated than the present and analogous to postal orders to be introduced.

19. Police officers in charge of stations to be empowered to inspect licenses of men found recruiting; but the police force otherwise to be forbidden under stringent orders from interfering with recruiting, save when called upon to do so in due course of law.

20. Directors or Assistant Directors of Agriculture to be made ex-officio local Protectors of Emigrants, and to be referred to for advice in cases of difficulty by the sub-agents up-country or by the Agents in Calcutta.

21. Magistrates and police officers to be enjoined to countenance and aid emigration to the best of their power.

22. The advantages likely to accrue in popularising emigration from all emigrants returning home so soon as entitled to a free passage to be passed on the colonies.

23. The grant of bonuses in land or rewards of other description to old emigrants on their re-emigrating, and being accompanied by relatives and neighbours, suggested.

24. Terms offered by various colonies to be painted or pasted on boards and hung up in the *tahsils* and *thanahs*.

25. Printed copies of such terms to be circulated freely to village officials and others, and a copy to be read to each batch of coolies at time of registration.

26. Detailed rules required for the guidance of registering officers in matters of doubt, such as age, claims made by guardians, cases of single women, &c.; in any case the employment of the police as a medium for enquiry strongly deprecated.

27. The *bhandara* system in Calcutta objected to, and payments in cash to coolies in lieu of kind suggested.

28. (1) Suggested that the pay and commission of subagents be fixed for all the colonies on one scale; (2) and that more than one sub-agent for the same agency be not allowed to recruit in the same district.

29. The plan proposed of only registering recruits in the district of domicile shown to be likely to hinder emigration and to bear very hard on certain sections of the population.

30. The advantages possessed by one colony as compared to another to be more clearly brought home to the people, so as to admit of the coolie making an intelligent choice.

31. Better railway accommodation pleaded for. Strict orders to railway police and servants to be issued regarding interference with coolies, and station-masters to be enjoined to help, as far as they can, recruits when in transit.

32. Certain precautions suggested regarding the medical examination of women, particularly women proceeding with their husbands.

33. That returning emigrants, if well conducted, should receive certificates from the colonial authorities.

34. Suggested that remittances from emigrants to their friends should always be paid over to the payee in the presence of the recruits in the local depot.

35. Proposed that plots of waste-land, where available, be allotted on favourable terms to returned emigrants proportionate to the capital possessed by such emigrant.

36. That the right of an adult woman to emigrate, if she chooses to do so, without reference to the wishes of her friends, be clearly recognised; and that enquiries from relatives through the police be discontinued.

NOTES

1. Natives have in some parts of the country a strong belief that in the colonies the coolies are suspended head downwards to facilitate the extraction of oil from them.
2. The rates for letters from India to Jamaica, Trinidad, Nevis, St Kitts, Guadeloupe, Martinique, St Croix, British Guiana and Suriname vary from 2 to 5 *annas,* 14 to Grenada, St Lucia and St Vincent, 9 to Natal and 6 to Fiji.

APPENDIX 1

Form of Agreement between the Agent and the Sub-agent

Trinidad Government Emigration Agency, 11 Garden Reach

To: , *Allahabad:*

Sir, You are appointed by the Government of Trinidad a Sub-Agent of Emigration during this season, subject to the following conditions.

1. The season commences on the—and closes on the day on which the last ship of the season leaves the port of Calcutta for —.

2. Males between the ages of twelve and thirty-five years of age and females between the ages of twelve and thirty, shall be considered statute adults. Two children from two to twelve years shall be deemed equivalent to one male statute adult. Infants under two years old shall not be taken into account.

3. Not less than forty female adults, pursuant to the minimum fixed by the Government of India, must accompany every hundred male adults; where this proportion is not fully maintained the right is reserved of rejecting emigrants, who will be sent back to their homes at the Sub-Agent's expense.

4. You will receive a monthly salary of Rs.—provided the number of statute adult emigrants passed and received into this depot as eligible monthly does not fall below—. In addition to this monthly stipend you will receive a further amount of Rs. 18 for each man and Rs. 28 for each woman to cover all expenses contingent on the collection, registration, train hire and way-expenses to the Government Emigration Depot at Garden Reach of each statute adult admitted and passed as eligible for emigration. This allowance, however, will not be granted

in the case of an emigrant who declines to emigrate, nor of any who are rejected after admission to the Depot, and the expenses in connection with the return of such emigrants to their homes will be charged to your account. Where desertions from the depot occur after five days have expired from the date of admission, Rs.—only will be paid in lieu of Rs.—, and nothing should they occur previously. Five days after the emigrants have been admitted to the depot and passed, you will receive Rs.—on account, and the remaining Rs.—after they embark for the colony. The rail-hire will be paid by means of the 'Credit notes' in general use, and debited, as already stated, to your account.

5. I need hardly remind you that you must act in strict accordance with the laws of India, especially No. VII. of 1871, and, above all, to see that your subordinates and recruiters deal fairly and honestly with intending emigrants. The advantages of emigration to Trinidad if clearly set before the people are so manifest, that, apart from the immorality of such a practice, no possible advantage can accrue either to the sub-agent or his subordinates by holding out expectations which they are aware will not be realised, for the intending emigrants are certain to be undeceived by the Agent and the Protector at Calcutta when categorically examined, even if they have failed clearly to realise their prospects when questioned by the Magistrate up-country, before whom they originally appeared to attest their desire to emigrate and have their names enrolled; for should they decline to proceed to the colony, you and your employees will forfeit all claim to any allowance for expenses contingent on collection, registration, and the journey to Calcutta.

6. A *per caput* fee of six *annas* will be paid for the district medical examination of all emigrants, the services of the District Civil Surgeon being enlisted where practicable.

The Surgeon who passes the people will certify the numbers, sex, &c., of those whom he has examined on the 'foil' and 'counterfoil' of the book provided for the purpose, and send the 'foil' to the sub-agent for transmission to Calcutta along with the emigrants. The Surgeon will also endorse on the back of the emigrants' certificates whether he considers them eligible or not.

7. Any further instructions or notice it may be considered necessary to issue should receive your immediate attention and be promptly acted on.

8. All recruiting licenses, printed forms, and brass badges will be supplied by the Agency free of charge, but other contingent expenses will be paid by the sub-agent.

Acting as Agent on behalf of the Government of—

APPENDIX 2

Form of Agreement between the Sub-agent and the Recruiter

Trinidad Emigration Sub-Agency
(A literal copy.)

Allahabad, 188 .

1st. I hereby agree to give you a contract for supplying intending emigrants for Trinidad during the season of 1880-81 from the districts and for supervising generally over their registration and other conveniences.

2nd. When the coolies are gathered by you, not under 10 men, I will have a *chalan* and you shall give a *chalan*, and I will have amongst 100 men 40 women, and if women and men are not sent, the rates will be decreased and then you will have to agree upon it, and when your coolies arrive here at Allahabad and are on the station (in the train) and arrive at Calcutta, then whatever may be your rates according to that your money will be *pakka*. If any coolie registered by the Doctor or by me run away or die or refuse at the time, the loss of which will be borne by you. Money you shall receive then when I will receive a letter from Calcutta saying all the coolies have arrived here safe: nothing will be paid for those under 10 years of age; over 12 you shall get half rate.

3rd. Rates for out districts: Fatehpur, each man, Rs. 6; each woman, Rs. 8. Banda, Mirzapur, and Beylah Partabgarh, the same if you wish to work at Allahabad; out villages the rates will be each man Rs. 6 and each woman Rs. 7; you will receive nothing of those that are under 12 years of age.

4th. All expenses for recruiting, registration, food for coolies, and other expenses up to the time of arrival at the station for down must be paid by you.

5th. Strong healthy field labourers are required and all such castes minor, whether male or female under 18 years of age will not be taken unless accompanied by respectable relatives or (father or mother). No men will be taken of soft hands or weak. 'Panjabis' are altogether refused. Men should be recruited of those sort when they agree to be vaccinated and also eat on board of ship.

6th. When you have taken the license of Trinidad and after which at any time without my license give the coolies elsewhere or have your license changed or send it by another man, and if made out there, whatever may be the rate of Calcutta I shall take from you, there will be no objection to it at all. Whatever this has been written if not done accordingly with License, and all, whatever may be the loss, it will all be taken from you and you will not hesitate at all.

Emigration Sub-Agent for Trinidad.
I agree to the terms and conditions of this agreement
Recruiter for Trinidad.

APPENDIX 3

Return showing by stations the total number of emigrants registered in the North-Western Provinces and Oudh during the four years (1878-1882)

No.	Station	No. of Emigrants Registered
1	Benares	5,064
2	Cawnpore	3,983
3	Lucknow	3,676
4	Fyzabad	3,201
5	Allahabad	3,007
6	Agra	2,748
7	Ghazipur	2,085
8	Bareilly	1,957
9	Muttra	1,928
10	Aligarh	1,744
11	Gorakhpur	1,697
12	Farukhabad	1,034
13	Azamgarh	734
14	Etawah	638
15	Basti	614
16	Mainpuri	603
17	Bulandahar	586
18	Gonda	508
19	Moradabad	500
20	Sultanpur	441
21	Jaunpur	363
22	Fatehpur	352
23	Unao	307
24	Shahjahanpur	300
25	Bara Banki	299
26	Meerut	260
27	Mirzapur	255
28	Hardoi	239

APPENDIX 3

29	Banda	228
30	Bahraich	175
31	Etah	166
32	Budaun	136
33	Sitapur	91
34	Partabgarh	59
35	Ballia	27
36	Rae Bareli	23
	TOTAL	40,028

NB. Including rejections by medical officers, deserters, and rejections by registering officers, the total number recruited was probably not less than 50,000.

APPENDIX 4

Notice to coolies intending to emigrate to British Guiana, generally called Demerara

You will be taken free of expense to Calcutta, and while there you will be well fed and properly lodged until the ship sails, and should you be ill the greatest care will be taken of you.

When the ship is ready you will be supplied with good clothing. The finest ships are selected, and the voyage takes about three months. The food, medicines and other appliances on board are of good quality and your health, comfort, and safety will be most carefully attended to. The Indian Government has appointed officers who are most strict and vigilant in securing for you all these advantages.

On your arrival in Demerara there are Government officials on purpose to advise and protect you, and at all times during your residence there, the greatest care and watchfulness is exercised by the Government of Demerara in seeing that all your rights and privileges are secured to you whether in health or in sickness.

Your religion is in no way interfered with, and both Hindus and Muhammadans are protected alike. You will find about 60,000 of your countrymen comfortably settled on the Sugar Plantations in Demerara, besides many more in towns and villages.

You will have a good house, rent-free, to live in, and the Protector of Immigrants in Demerara will take care that you are not overcrowded or separated from your relatives.

You will have plenty of garden ground to cultivate at your leisure.

The climate of Demerara is never so hot or so cold as in India, and suits your countrymen, and you will find an abundance of fresh water, fruits, and vegetables.

If you wish to write or remit money to your friends in India, the Protector will always be glad to direct you in sending such letters or money-orders through the Agent here.

You will be required to cultivate sugarcane and to make sugar, rum, and molasses. Great varieties of work, either for strong men, or for women and children, are always abundantly available, and the amount of money earned depends on the strength and experience of the labourer; upwards of eighty *lakhs* of rupees are paid yearly as wages to different classes of labourers; certain works is done by the day, but most is *thika* or task-work. Minimum daily wage, eight *annas* for able-bodied males of and above fifteen; and five *annas* four *pies* for adult males not able-bodied or for males of and above ten and under fifteen, or for all females of and above ten. There are many kinds of works at which more may be earned after the emigrant has had practice and experience. In the Sugar Factory, for instance:

Boiling Sugar	18-21 *annas* a day
Making fire under the Boiler	13-16 ditto
Feeding mill with canes	11-16 ditto
Removing crushed canes	11-13 ditto
Potting Sugar	11-13 ditto
Curing Sugar	11-13 ditto

In the cane-field, *thika* work, such as digging trenches, shovel ploughing or cutting canes, is paid for at higher rates than lighter works, such as weeding or picking up cane-trash. Your countrymen in Demerara own live-stock worth upwards of thirteen *lacs* of *rupees*, jewellery worth six *lacs* of rupees, besides money in the Savings' Bank and other properties amounting to nearly thirty *lacs* of rupees. After five years' industrial residence you may return to India at your own expense. So soon as you shall have earned Rs. 758 either by time or by task-work, your indenture shall absolutely cease and be determined notwithstanding the term of five years being unexpired. After ten years you are entitled to a free passage back to India. Over thirteen thousand of your countrymen returned in twenty-five years, bringing with them over twenty-six *lacs* of *rupees* in cash, besides jewellery valued at nearly five *lacs*.

For three months after your arrival your employer will feed you with good wholesome food at a charge of two *annas* eight *pies* a day and according to the following scale for each adult:

	Chittacks	Kancha
Rice	4	-
Dal	1½	-
Cocoanut oil or Ghi	½	-
Masala	-	1½
Sugar	1	-

	Seer
Yams, Plantains, Sweet Potatoes,	1
Tannias, Cassava, or Cornmeal Flour	½

When you have a knowledge of the habits and customs of Demerara, and have your own provision garden, besides cows and goats of your own, you may live well at a cost of about 2½ *annas* a day.

Females will find immense advantages. Those who are married will be fully protected, and those who wish to marry will have excellent offers from their well-to-do countrymen. Throughout British Guiana, the women are generally laden with gold or silver ornaments. Females, when pregnant or suckling children are not required to work.

H. A. FIRTH,
Emigration Agent for Govt. of British Guiana
8, Garden Reach,
Calcutta, 1881

APPENDIX 5

Statement showing distribution by residence of the emigrants from the North-Western Provinces and Oudh, for the year 1881-82, and exhibiting the proportionate amount of emigration from each district

No.	District	Pop. Census, 1881	Actual no. of emigrants
1	Agra	974,892	620
2	Muttra	871,105	424
3	Aligarh	1,019,864	487
4	Mainpuri	799,871	374
5	Sultanpur	956,695	386
6	Fatehpur	683,389	248
7	Etawah	722,071	255
8	Lucknow	796,329	240
9	Rae Bareli	952,059	322
10	Allahabad	1,473,550	446
11	Shahjahanpur	856,169	262
12	Fyzabad	1,117,419	302
13	Bareilly and Pilibhi	1,028,987	273
14	Jaunpur	1,207,086	305
15	Etah	755,530	192
16	Partabgarh	845,685	195
17	Cawnpore	1,173,215	267
18	Bara Banki	1,027,188	205
19	Gonda	1,267,422	236
20	Ghazipur and Ballia	1,673,572	293
21	Benares	919,482	157
22	Bulandahahr	924,442	154
23	Farukhabad	905,661	137
24	Basti	1,627,712	233
25	Azamgarh	1,602,036	239
26	Unao	894,505	131

27	Budaun	903,021	129
28	Bahraich	876,650	121
29	Meerut	1,314,301	136
30	Mirzapur	1,140,501	125
31	Moradabad	1,151,394	112
32	Hardoi	987,789	93
33	Banda	700,929	43
34	Jalaun	417,882	26
35	Saharanpur	978,603	52
36	Bijnor	721,265	43
37	Sitapur	959,487	42
38	Gorakhpur	2,605,100	102
39	Muzaffarnagar	758,215	24
40	Jhansi	382,518	12
41	Kheri	826,400	18
42	Kumaun	494,636	7
43	Garhwal	343,650	-
44	Tarsai	207,161	-
45	Dehra Dun	143,592	-
46	Hamirpur	507,021	-
47	Lalitpur	248,802	-
	TOTAL	43,595,662	8,469

APPENDIX 6

Extracts from Correspondence. From Emigration Agent for Demerara, dated 30th March, 1882.

Four years ago I addressed the British Guiana Government on the subject of remittances and postal communication, and now enclose a copy of No. 1254, dated 26th March, 1879.

When I left Demerara for Calcutta in 1872, I was aware that few of the emigrants in the colony kept up communication by letter with their friends in India, and that none ever thought of remitting money.

A small beginning in this direction was made in 1873, which has very slowly developed up to last year when 144 letters were received through this office from coolies in Demerara, and 75 were forwarded to Demerara. This, 1 take it, represents pretty nearly all the correspondence that passed during that year between the natives of India and their relatives in British Guiana.

The enclosed register shows the sum total remitted to Calcutta from Demerara by coolies exclusive of the large sums brought by return emigrants.

		Rs.	annas	pice
1873	2 remittances	51	0	0
1874	5 do.	336	0	0
1875	7 do.	1,034	2	0
1876	10 do.	625	15	6
1877	12 do.	2,168	11	6
1878	37 do.	2,217	7	1

The importance of encouraging, by every means available, an exchange of news between the coolies in the west and those in the east cannot in the interests of emigration be over-estimated.

***

Extract from letter addressed to the British Guiana Government by the Emigration Agent, n.d.

With a view of furthering to some extent this two-fold object, vie., the promotion of emigration hence to Demerara, and the permanent settlement of those in the colony, I have the honor to submit, for His Excellency the Governor's consideration, a scheme for facilitating, as far as practicable, the transmission of letters and money from the coolie emigrants in British Guiana to their friends (in India).

1st   The fact to be published and circulated as widely as possible amongst the coolies, that letters and money can be safely transmitted by them to their friends in India, through the Immigration Department.

2nd   The Sub-Immigration Agents to forward weekly to the Immigration Agent-General whatever letters and remittances they may collect in the district, and, with each remittance, to fill in a Remittance Order leaving the No. blank.

3rd   A register to be kept at the Georgetown Immigration Office containing only an index of the particulars shown in the enclosed register, as may be necessary.

4th   Each Remittance Order to be numbered when entered in the register.

5th   A Colonial Bank Bill of exchange at short sight on London for the amount in sterling to be transmitted with the Remittance Orders to this office by the next following mail.

6th   A register to be kept here in the form enclosed with the remittance orders entered consecutively in proper sequence by their colonial number.

7th   A copy of this register to be forwarded yearly for the purpose of comparing and checking it with the register kept in the colony.

My reason for the fifth suggestion is that these Bills, with the present depreciated value of the *rupee*, can be readily sold here at a considerable profit to the payee.

APPENDIX 6

From Emigration Agent for Demerara, dated 9th June, 1882.

I have heard nothing more about the correspondence and remittance scheme.

APPENDIX 7

List of Castes in the North-Western Provinces, 1881

Name of Caste	General Occupation
Agar (or Agaria)	Saltpetre, salt maker, iron worker
Ahar	Cultivator
Ahir	Cattle breeder, milk seller, cultivator
Arakh	Village service, cultivator
Badi	Cultivator, dancing, singing
Badiphul	Oilmaker
Bahelia	Fowler
Bahrupia	Actor
Bajgi	Musician
Bulahar	Village messenger
Balahi	Brickmaker
Balai	Weaver
Bandi	Drummer, bird trapper
Bania	Trader, money lender, banker
Banjara	Travelling grain dealer
Banmanas	Rope, string, and mat maker
Bansphor	Bamboo worker
Baona	Cattle dealer
Bargi	Service, cultivation, shikari
Bargah (or Bargahi)	Service, leaf plate maker
Barhai	Carpenter
Barhia	Edge tool sharpener
Bari	Leaf plate seller, torch bearer
Barwar	Grass cutter, seller
Bawaria	Cultivator, thief
Bayar	Cultivator, field labourer, earth digger
Beohara	Money lender
Bhantu	Thief

APPENDIX 7

Bhangi	Sweeper
Bhar	Agriculture
Bharthi	Beggar
Bhat	Ballad singer
Bhotia	Agriculture, labour, commerce
Bhumihar	Land holder and cultivator
Bhurji	Grain parcher
Bhurtia	Cultivator
Bilwar (or Belwari)	Grain dealer and cultivator
Bind	Toddy-drawer, cultivator
Birjbasi	Dancing, singing
Bogsha	Agriculture
Boria	Village servant, cultivator
Bot	Cultivator, labourer
Brahman	Agriculturist, minister of Hindoo religion
Bunkar	Cloth weaver
Chai	Fisherman
Chamar	Leather worker, labourer
Charaj	Assistant at Hindoo Funeral obsequies
Chauhan	Agriculturist, landowner
Cheru	Cultivator
Chharu	Mat weaver
Chhera	Sweeper
Chhipi	Calico printer
Dabgar	Leather vessel (kuppa) maker
Dalera	Day labourer, thief
Dangi	Agriculture
Darzi	Tailor
Dhandhor	See Ahir
Dhanuk	Village messenger, watchman
Dharwal	Dancing and singing
Dhingar	Cultivator, excavator
Dhobi	Washerman
Dhuna	Cotton carder
Dom	Bamboo basket maker, singing and dancing
Fakir	Religious ascetic, beggar
Gadaria	Sheep and goat breeder, wool spinner
Gamela	Agriculture

Gandharp	Dancing and singing
Gandhi	Scent seller
Gandhila	Agriculture and catching wild animals
Gharuk	Agriculture, fishing and service
Ghogh	Rope maker
Ghosi	Milkman, cultivator
Gokain	Worker in wood
Gorcha	Fishing and mat making
Gorkha	Service
Gujar	Landholder and agriculturist
Gushain	Devotee, saint
Habura	Cultivator, thief, shikari
Halwai	Confectioner
Jaiswar	Grass cutter, shoemaker
Jat	Cultivator
Joria	Day labourer, weaver
Joshi	Service, receiver of alms
Julaha	Weaver
Kachhar	Cultivator
Kachhi	Gardener, field labourer
Kachhwa	Market gardener
Kadhar	Boatman
Kahar	Palanquin bearer, water carrier
Kalwa	Distiller
Kamangar	House painter
Kamboh	Cultivator
Kanchan	Dancer, prostitute
Kandu	Cultivator, shopkeeper
Kanjar	Rope maker, trapper
Kaparia	Beggar
Karar	Cultivator, labourer
Karnatak	Rope dancer
Karol	Shoemaker
Kasera	Metal vessel dealer
Kasondhan	Trader
Katwa	Yarn spinner, calico printer, weaver
Kathyara	Bricklayer
Kayasth	Clerk

Khagi	Agriculture, labour, domestic service
Khangar	Watching, theft
Kharkata	Grass cutter
Kharot	Mat weaver
Khairwara	Cultivation and general labour
Khatik	Butcher
Khairna	Cultivation and labour
Khattri	Commerce, service
Kolapuri	Trader
Kori	Weaver
Kuta	Rice husker
Kotamali	Grain seller
Kotwar	Cultivation
Kumhar	Potter
Kunjra	Greengrocer
Kurmi	Landholder, cultivator
Lodha	Landholder, cultivator
Lohar	Blacksmith
Lonia	Excavator, field labourer, saltpetre maker
Maha Brahman	Performer of funeral ceremonies of Hindoos
Mal	Landowner, cultivator
Mali	Gardener
Mallah	Boatman
Manihar	Glass bangle maker, seller
Meo	Cultivator, cattle breeder
Nai	Barber
Nalband	Farrier
Nat	Acrobat
Natak	Dancer
Nayak	Cultivators, traders, prostitutes
Negpatar	Attendant of prostitutes
Niaria	Gold and silversmiths' waste washer
Orh	Trader
Paheri	Cultivator, village watchman
Paria	Beggar
Pasi	Village watchman, cultivator
Pasia	Cultivator and field labourer
Pattiar	Cultivator, landowner

Patwa	Braid, fringe, tape maker
Pahri or Parahia	Cultivation, labour and service
Purbia	Excavator, labourer
Ramaiya	Pedlar
Raj	Mason
Rajbhat	Cultivation
Rajbhar	Cultivation, pig keeping
Rajput	Cultivator
Rangaswami	Fortune teller
Rangrez	Dryer
Rastogi	Cloth merchant and money lender
Rawa	Agriculture
Rehti	Money lending
Riwari	Agriculture
Ronia	Trade and cultivation
Saharia	Cultivator, labourer, trapper
Saikalgar	Metal polisher
Sangher	Fisherman and water nut grower
Sangtarash	Stone quarrier and cutter
Sapera	Snake charmer
Sejwari	Service
Setwar	Cultivator
Soiri	Cultivator
Son	Labourer
Sunar	Goldsmith
Sunkar	Excavator
Taga	Landholder, cultivator
Tamoli	Betel leaf seller
Tarikash	Toddy-drawer
Tarkihar	'Tarki' maker
Tatwa	Cultivator and palanquin bearer
Tawaif	Dancer, prostitute
Teli	Oilmaker
Tharu	Cultivation
Thathera	Brass and coppersmith
Tirgar	Bow and arrow maker
Turha	Palanquin bearer
Turi (Toria)	Basket maker, coolie*

*See India Office Library, S/974, Census of India, 1881. Although not part of Major Pitcher's Report, this Appendix is included in the study largely for reference purposes since, as clearly indicated in the text, emigrants from the region comprised various caste groups. In 1881 the population of the North-Western Provinces was an estimated 38,053,304, the largest castes numerically being *Chamars, Brahmans* and *Ahirs*.

Diary of tour in the North-Western Provinces and Oudh while on Special Duty in connection with emigration to the Colonies from British India

March 6th – Gave over charge of the Small Cause Court on the afternoon of the 6th, and in consequence of a telegram from Major Erskine, Commissioner of Sitapur, asking me to join him in camp and inspect the locality where it was proposed, if possible, to locate some returned emigrants. I left by the evening train for Shajahanpur. From the latter station I wrote to Major Erskine's camp at Mohumdi. Arriving there on the morning of the 7th in time to march on with him to Muhammadpur, where we halted for the day.

Read over the long and rather intricate file of correspondence connected with the drainage of the Kutna Valley, and the settling of the waste lands on the banks of the Kutna under the scheme proposed by Colonel MacAndrew, formerly Commissioner of the Division. The Executive Engineer in charge of the drainage works and the Deputy Commissioner in charge of the waste lands were both in camp, and I discussed details with them.

March 8th – The camp moved by direct road to Bhikampur, while the Commissioner, Deputy Commissioner, Executive Engineer, and myself made a detour round by the Government lands in question, and after having thoroughly inspected them and made local enquiries, we returned to camp by evening, taking our route along the line of drainage works.

As regards the grants, what we found was this:

There are two small 'grants' of a total area of 485 acres upon which it is proposed to commence as an experiment.

In the centre of each about an acre has been cleared upon which the *abddi* is to be located, and from which roads are to radiate in various directions to the border of each grant or village.

In the centre of each *abddi* a good masonry well for the supply of good drinking water, the first essential to successful colonisation of jungle land, is under process of construction, and these wells will, if expedition be used, be completed this hot season. So far there is but one family located on the land, that of a *Lunia*, to whom has been entrusted the construction of the wells, and his house has only just been commenced.

We were surrounded by a lot of *Thakurs* from a neighbouring village who were very anxious to obtain lots: but it appeared on cross-questioning the leading man that he had for a long time held waste land in another grant of which he had only brought a very small portion under cultivation, having no doubt insufficient capital.

There are registered applications for the whole of the land, but in no case so far, is it believed, that the applicant has sufficient available capital.

On our return we were enabled to see the drainage works, which appear to be effecting the object sought. It was strange though to see the amount of *reh* in some part of this jungle which has never been cultivated, and in making fresh cuttings for the river, beds of *reh* are found underlying apparently good soil.

We passed through many grants larger and better than the Government grants with but very little cultivation. It only requires capital and liberal terms to tenants to turn the whole of these grants into cultivated land. The Kutua could be bunded at various points of its course to afford a constant water-supply.

March 9th – Marched from Bhikampur to Kaimara. Drew out forms of *patta* and *kabuliyat*.

March 10th – Marched from Kaimara to Kheri and then drove in the 80 miles or so to Lucknow.

March 11th – At Lucknow; letters from and to emigration agents; read emigration proceedings.

March 12th – Sunday.

March 13th – Letters to emigration agents about offering leases to emigrants returning ex *Sylhet* and other ships; read correspondence; wrote to Assistant Secretary and to Deputy Commissioner and Commissioner at Kheri.

March 14th – Wrote to Secretary, North-Western Provinces, asking for copy of bill and correspondence. At the Lucknow *kutcherry* all day, examining emigration registers[1] and copying out the addresses of emigrants whose houses lay in villages in the Mohanlalganj. Took two volumes of the register out into camp with me, and moved out into camp at Bukas, eight miles from Lucknow.

Found that the corpse of a man, who had died of cholera some 7 or 8 miles away, had been brought to the village during the day, and that a resident of the village had since been taken ill also with cholera. This is the fourth instance I can cite within my own personal knowledge where the practice of carrying cholera corpses back to the village, instead of burying them at the place where death occurred, has been followed by other cases in the village to which they have been so brought back.

Results of examination of Lucknow registers – Register in form as laid down by circular, of ample size and strongly bound, carefully written, and names of people and places, as a rule, spelt correctly.

The book is signed by the Magistrate, and the required certificate to the effect that the registration and examination of the emigrants has been conducted according to Government orders duly appended.

The names of all those presented for registration are entered in the register, and the Magistrate, having erased with his own hand the names of those who may refuse to go or of those whom he may for some reason or other refuse to register, enters in the certificate the exact number passed.

A foot-note is then made by the clerk of the amount of fees received, and he also notes the date on which he despatches copy of the register to the Protector of Emigrants and to the Emigration Agent.

The column headed 'number' seems to be filled in in a very unsystematic way; sometimes the series runs for a quarter, sometimes for a month.

The column headed 'depot to which to proceed' is invariably filled in as 'Calcutta.' I find a great diversity of practice in districts as regards the serial number and depot column. In some the serial number runs for the year, in others for the quarter, in others for the month, while in some the year commences from January, others select April, and others again June.

Some enter Calcutta for the depot, while others enter Demerara, Trinidad, Fiji, &c., as the case may be.

The column for 'occupation' is invariably, I may say, filled in with either 'cultivator' or 'labourer,' but latterly I find that it has been omitted altogether from the Lucknow register, and I think rightly so, as it does not matter much what trade a man followed, so long as he is willing and able to perform field labour, which is all that he is required to do.

Here and there the number of names struck out as refused registration one day exceeds the number struck out on succeeding days in a way that can only, I fear, be the result of temper or *Hakim-ke-mizaj*, a phrase which I hear but too frequently in the course of my enquiries.

Sometimes the names are struck out and no reason assigned.

Here are some of the reasons assigned copied verbatim and dated 1871.

'The names of Wahid Khan (18 years of age in register), Musammat Bhulia, Musammat Mohunia and Musammat Muna, Nidhi (18), and Imam Ali (19), are cut out, as small boys cannot go without their father's leave, nor should wives go without husbands' permission.'

The ages of the 'boys' so called are noted as above in the register; and in the column of next-of-kin Imam Ali is noted as having a mother, but no father. All the women give as heirs or next-of-kin the names of relatives other than husbands, though where a woman has a husband it is usual to give his name as *Waris*. Two of the women had children with them.

The batch in the register next to the above went before another officer for registration, who passed all the women brought before him and remarks: 'The women without husbands say they are widows.'

From register for 1879: 'Women will be seen to hereafter not registered.' Next day against another lot is written: 'Case as to women will be enquired into:' and a little further on: 'Recruiter says the women he does not want; names erased.'

Considering that the recruiter has to pay the cost of feeding the women pending such vague enquiries, it is not surprising that he should have withdrawn their names. In all probability some of these women were widows who had lost their husbands during the scarcity of 1877-78.

'This mark x (against several women) signifies stopped for enquiry,' and the mark appears very frequently afterwards.

A remark – 'Not fit to emigrate,' but no further explanation given.

'These women not passed, as enquiry must be made about them, as they come from other districts.'

'Those cut out (4) are from other districts, and enquiries about their husbands are to be made.'

'The woman from Aligarh cut out.'

The woman above alluded to was a *Bhat* and had two small children with her, aged 7 and 2 1/2. After nearly a month she was allowed to emigrate, on the Magistrate of Aligarh reporting that no one claimed her.

With a view to tracing out the families and addresses given of emigrants who had left the Lucknow, Rae Bareli, and Sultanpur districts, through which I proposed to make a tour, I copied out that day a great number of names; but eventually, with the permission of the Deputy Commissioner, carried off into camp the old registers up to 1879.

March 15th – Camp Bukas. Moved out into camp yesterevening selecting the Mohanlalganj *tahsil* as a commencement; the *lambardars* being, as a rule, personally known to me, and therefore the less likely to misinterpret the object of my enquiry.

Took a list of addresses of coolies who had been registered as belonging to villages in the vicinity. Visited Ansari Khera, the village of one Khushial, *Chamar,* who was registered in 1868.

On first enquiry no one seemed to recollect Khushial. Went to the house of Prag Singh, *Thakur* and *lambardar* of the village, an old acquaintance of mine, and had a long conversation with him, while the usual bowl of milk, which politeness necessitates one's drinking, was being got ready.

Prag Singh seemed familiar enough with 'emigration' said that it was only dread of the unknown which deterred people from the journey, coupled with which was a general impression that emigrants became *Bedharam* from being forced to eat out of one dish on boardship, along with people of other castes, and also that on arrival at the colonies they were forcibly converted to Christianity.

Had heard of Jia Lal, *Pasi,* having returned from some place to the village of Chaurasi (about a mile distant) and of his having left again.

By this time the *chaukidar* having evidently satisfied himself that my intentions were not sinister, said that he remembered Khushial returning stone-blind after having been absent for three years, and then wandering away from the village to beg for a livelihood.

Rode on to Chaurasi, where again the *chaukidar* at first professed complete ignorance of Jia Lal and his belongings, and only when quite assured that no harm was intended either to the emigrant's relatives or to himself did he admit that he knew the man. He then stated that Jia Lal, after having been registered at Lucknow along with his family, had gone off to Calcutta, but after a short time returned and again left as a registered emigrant. At first sight there appeared to have been some fraud perpetrated on the agencies; subsequently, on returning to camp, I found that on 18th January, 1878, Jia Lal with his wife, son, and daughter-in-law, were registered for Demerara, while on 28th May, 1878, the same four people under an identical description were registered for Surinam. I at once wrote to the Calcutta Agency for Demerara, and found that Jia Lal and his relatives were rejected in Calcutta and sent back to their homes as being physically unfit. Doubtless by May they had recovered condition sufficiently (it was during the scarcity) to be acceptable to the Surinam Agency. The fact of this family persisting thus in emigrating speaks well for the care taken of coolies from the time of engagement to the time of embarkation.

Once and for all I may here remark that in many subsequent instances I still further had before me in evidence the studied ignorance of villagers regarding coolies who had emigrated until assured that acquaintance with their names or families was fraught with no evil consequence to any one. And this fact shows the inadvisability of making enquiries through the police a test as to whether a woman who has been brought up for registration has given a correct address or not. As a rule, the police seem to report that nothing is known of the woman at the address given, whereas after testing some hundreds of cases I have found scarcely one where the address was not correct, and of this my next visit gave me a good example. I rode on from Chaurasi, accompanied by the *chaukidar,* towards Misa, assured by my guide that we should pass no village from whence any coolie had gone. Passing Bazupur, however, I spoke to a man reaping in the fields, who proved to be the *chaukidar,* and heard that a man had emigrated from the village, so I turned aside and in the *lambardars* Isram Singh and Ajudhia Singh, Chandel *Thakurs,* found again old acquaintances. Bhawna, *Pasi,* had emigrated in *Jet,* 1878, during the scarcity. He had gone to Lucknow, sending from there a message to his wife and son that he was off to Demerara and would return in five years. The wife and son were still in the village, earning their living by ordinary *mazduri;* but although only four years had elapsed the woman was tired of waiting and was about to marry some one else despite all remonstrances. Would I kindly see the woman and remonstrate with her? So she was brought up and admonished to wait until I could, if possible, procure news of her husband, which I undertook to do. I must say that the woman looked rather sulky at her little plan being interrupted[2], and it seemed quite a new idea to the village generally that a man should either return, or return bringing money with him, though they held to the idea that a return after five years was always promised.

As no man from Bazupur appeared in the register I was rather puzzled, and on return to camp at 11 a.m. copied out the addresses of several men of the same name for further enquiry.

Took also the following remarks from the register, dated 3rd November, 1871:

"The men say that they have entered into agreements with Bhawani and Safdar Ali, the recruiters. The recruiters denied having any bonds. I decline to pass one of these persons. Moreover, I call on Safdar Ali and Bhawanidin to show me their instructions, according to which they have promised Rs. 104 besides a free passage. Also that there will be only five hours' work."[3] In 1872 and following years coolies are struck out as 'not approved'; 'does not appear more than 14;' also 186 men struck out in October, 1872 with 'not approved: they have wives and children at home,' an entry which occurs several times. Against another is written: 'I have summoned the woman's husband. He has abandoned her and has taken up with another woman. He said he did not care where she went. She wants to go, as she won't live with her husband. I did not pass her last time (24th September, 1872) pending these inquiries; I see no reason now for keeping her.' (29th October, 1872). Also in November, 1872 nine men are struck out of a batch bracketed with the remarks 'Not approved for various reasons, or absent when called to-day.'

Six are struck out of a batch in January, 1873, and bracketed as follows:

    1258)
    1305) Must bring their sons.

    1275)

1276) Don't want to go.

1290)
1291) Rejected.

A remark in 1879: – 'I have disallowed No. 132 aged 17, on the application of his uncle, who says that he is the only support of his old parents.'

No. 138 (a woman aged 35, with a son aged 10) disallowed, as she has a husband in service at Partabgarh.

P.M. – Rode to Daudnagar. On the way at Bharkhambha, found the relatives of *Pasis* who had gone off with their families, fleeing from the scarcity of 1878. The villagers had tried to prevent these families from leaving. Complaints made of having received no news of the emigrants 'since they went to China.'

At Daudnagar a *Pasi* who emigrated 15 years ago had never been heard of again. Another *Pasi* left in 1878, and a *fakir* (by caste) last year: no news of them. Heard here that a *Pasi* had lately returned to a village some 6 or 7 miles away after many years of absence, and bringing with him a Thakurain as wife and plenty of money. He is still out of caste on account of the strange woman, whom he alleges to have been sold to him, and his stories generally seem to have much scandalised the countryside. Just by accident I heard of a *Brahmin* living in Adampur Bharkhambha who had returned from Demerara, but of whose existence the Bharkambha *Pasis* had made no mention, though living close by.

Devi Singh of Daudnagar promised to bring the *Brahmin* to my tents next day.

March 16th – To Bazupur, to make further enquiries about Bhawania. Was much entertained on the way by traditions of Baka's history.

The position is shown of a large well, said to have been made by the *Bhars*, and into which the bodies of the dead were thrown during some terrible famine. A depression in the ground marks the site, and the *chaukidar* gravely assured me that annually, on the morning of the Diwali, a sow and five young ones are seen to issue from the ground at this spot. During the *Nawabi*, a diviner or *Buhsanga* once offered 8 or 9 *lakhs* of *rupees* for permission to search the ruins of the old *Bhar* fort for treasure, but was refused.

At Bazupur found that Bhawan was indentical with Bhawania, son of Jedha, resident of Degarria, of the register; Jedha being really his grandfather's name, and Degarria the village in which he was born and had lived for a long time. It adjoins Bazupur and the name of Bhawania's son had been given correctly in the next-of-kin column, so there would have been practically no difficulty in tracing him from his address.

On to, Misa, whence several men had emigrated: addresses all correct; no news of any of them.

On to Jehangirpur, the *lambardars* being well known to me. This village was lightly assessed and the people hold together. Could not hear of any one having left. Was told a tale how two or three years ago a woman was heard crying for help out on the sandy waste near the village. The villagers went to her assistance and found her with a man, a recruiter[4] of coolies travelling to Lucknow. Her story was that the man had lured her from her village[5] under a promise of keeping her, but that on their halting at Gosainganj for the night, he never went near her all night. This made her suspicious and led her to cry for help as she had done. The parties were taken to the *thana*, and on enquiry the woman, who had two or three small children with her, was sent back to her home.

At noon Ganga Din Misr of Adampur, the returned emigrant from Demerara, came to see me and tell his story which he did in a very amusing way.

His crops had failed in 1868, and unable any longer to withstand the taunts of his wife's people, who said that his family was starving, he slipped out one evening with two *annas* and an old blanket, saying he was going to see some one in a neighbouring village, and made his way to Lucknow. Met an acquaintance in the *bazaar*, who, finding that Ganga Din was in search of work, recommended him to the depot, where he got another two *annas* and so was able to have a good meal and go to sleep. On awaking he thought of going outside, but was stopped, and told that it was for his good that he should not go into the *bazaar*, as the people would tell him lies. Gave a curious account of his voyage: how he went not only over the *kala pani*, but also a sufait, lal, nila, and hara pani. Described St. Helena and the terror of the coolies at sea in a storm: how some of them used to cry. Highly eulogised the good and plentiful food on board. Was very happy in Berbice, but got into a scrape over some woman, who made away with Rs. 250 of his.

Plenty of food; water particularly good: the only fault in the climate, the prevalence of east winds leading to lumbago. Everybody made to work and not allowed to idle. Far greater truth and honesty amongst the coolies than in Hindustan. A general idea that woman grow younger and prettier after arrival. The character of the women, as a rule, so loose as to form one of the only drawbacks. Another small drawback is the prevalence of *jiggahs* (the flesh-burrowing tick of the West Indies). Negroes and Dutchmen held in great contempt, but the 'Dutchmen' so called are probably Creoles.

The reasons why people do not write or remit are:

1. Heavy postage and heavy charges of remittance.
2. The untrustworthiness of the Negro postmen, who are credited with destroying letters.[6]

No difficulty in getting a letter written, as there are always Hindustani writers in the offices.

Allowed to clear jungle and hold it rent-free for a time. Very large fish, and in plenty, to be had at any time in the drainage channels of the estates for the trouble of catching them. The same amount of clothing worn all the year round. Many men very well off: some wealthy. A coolie (from Ghazipur) bought an estate and engaged coolies on his own account, but the European planters, having grown jealous of him, combined to prevent his sugar being sold in London last year, and he was ruined (the latter part I subsequently heard from two recently returned coolies at Benares).

Trinidad supposed to be better than Demerara; one defect of the latter, by the way, being the prevalence of ghosts.

Does not think that men would care to take their families so long as the arrangements regarding women remain as at present. Paid his own passage to Calcutta, and arrived in Lucknow with Rs. 500 in notes and some cash. Treated himself to a ride in an *ekka,* in which he arrived in state in his village, to the astonishment of his wife and two children after an absence of some 7 or 8 years. Invested in land, cattle and carts. Paid off his wife's liabilities and settled down. Took a *lambardarship* of opium, but owing to the unfavourable seasons of the last 4 or 5 years had not done well, and was now thinking of going to Bombay for work; was very thankful when I engaged him as a *chaprasi,* as I did.

He told me also how the *chaukidar* of the village, observing his wealth and some jackets and pantaloons of European cut, which had been issued for boardship use, went off to the *thana* to report that 'a Brahmin had returned to the village after murdering a *Subadar* and stealing his money and uniform.' Thereupon orders were given, to arrest the emigrant and bring him with the property to the *thana.* On the road the *chaukidar* made an offer to let him go for two *rupees*, which, however, the emigrant declined, and at the *thana* succeeded in convincing the *thanadar* of the falsity of the report. The *chaukidar* then became curious about Demerara, and in the end emigrated along with his wife and small children, a married son and the wife of the latter also accompanying him. This subsequently proved from the Lucknow register to be quite true: only instead of going to Demerara the *chaukidar's* party got into a batch for Jamaica.

Mentioning the above story to the Collector of Etawah, the latter informed me that many years ago, when in the Ghazipur district, the police came to him in great excitement to say that they had arrested a party of *dacoits* in possession of a large quantity of loot. The supposed *dacoits* when brought to the Magistrate's tents, proved to be a party of emigrants on the way to their homes from the Mauritius with, a very large sum of money in their possession in dollars, the uncanny look of which appeared to have raised doubts in the *thanadar's* mind. Of course the party were at once released and their property tendered to them, but, it then being evening, they refused to take it and insisted on the Collector keeping it for them till the morning, which he was forced to do in his own tent, to the great disturbance of his peace of mind.

March 17th – Moved camp to Gosainganj, and on the way wandered round Patharnagar to Bhutwara, Sathwara, Beli, and Majgawan, in all of which I found old acquaintances amongst the *zamindars*. At Bhutwara they said that no one had emigrated, though the register showed three or four names, and I have not since been able to indentify these latter; they probably belong to Bhutwara in the Lucknow *tahsil* and constitute one of the few instances where the address given was not correct in any particular.

From Sathwara several *Chamars* and *Pasis* had left, some leaving families and others taking their families with them; no news since leaving and the families left working on at daily labour. At Beli also two had left. From Majgaon a *Pasi* emigrated 16 or 17 years ago, and nothing more having been heard of him, the wife (whom I saw) had married again. I found in these villages an idea that the emigrants went to China, and on asking them where they supposed that the opium, which was growing all round, went, they promptly replied: 'Oh, everybody knows that it goes to the country the people of which have heads like horses and make broadcloth.'

In the evening rode to Chand Sarai. Khimiah, *Chamarin*, who appears in the register as accompanied by some small children, had after her husband's death taken two *rupees* and set off for Lucknow to go to *Mirch*,[7] leaving one daughter to be taken care of by her relatives. The girl has since married. At Korehwa, an adjoining village, Nanku, *Chamar*, told me that his daughter Mohania had been turned out of home by her husband, who had taken up with another woman; she then went to Lucknow and was recruited for *Mirch*. Nanku, hearing of this, visited her at the depot and offered to pay for her food and to take her back, but she refused to give up the idea of emigrating.

Met a *Pasi* on the road who told me that one relative of his had gone off along with a family and another without his family. The man eagerly enquired if I could get news of these people.

At Chand Sarai I found the *zamindars* with all their *gurh* on their hands. Their Mahajan refused to take it at the price originally stipulated for when he made advances. It having been a particularly good season, he could afford to keep the *zamindars* waiting in the hopes of beating them down, and it was no use trying to sell to another *Mahajan*, as trade custom binds down other traders not to purchase until the man who first advanced money on the crop is satisfied.

March 18th – Visited Gouria and Likania in the morning. Interviewed a *Bania* named Dhune, whose family had long resided at Gosainganj and had property there. He had for some months been engaged in supplying with food the recruits collected by Gungadin, a licensed recruiter, who had left when the season for Trinidad closed. Dhune explained that on account of the high road from Lucknow to Sultanpur running through the Ganj it was a very good place for recruits. Wayfarers in search of work were accosted, and the villages were never visited. Women are, he told me, regularly employed to recruit coolie women near Lucknow and other large towns. The man seemed to have no idea of anything being wrong in employing women to recruit. He had applied for a license for himself, but had got no reply, and he was certainly a sharp, intelligent, and probably solvent man, who would make a far better recruiter than many of the men I have seen. Said that the women employed got their food and half an *anna* a day, besides Re. 1 to Rs. 2 for every recruit brought.

In the evening rode to Mullowli, from whence three young girls (sisters) had emigrated. When starving in 1878 their father had deserted them, but since the seasons ended he has returned and is employed in the Sajji works.

Puran, *Pasi*, anxiously enquired for his son Bakhtawar, who was registered in 1878.

Whatever may be the result of my tour, I at least shall retain a strong feeling of satisfaction at the recollection of the evident gratitude of many of these poor people to hear from me that relatives whom they had long given up as dead might yet be alive and well, and might possibly either return or be communicated with.

March 19th – Moved camp. Rode round by Shewar and identified addresses given, but found no relatives left. The same at Raipur and Simra, save that at the latter place the father of one emigrant was still in the village. On by Sithauli to Khujauli, from whence quite a large number had emigrated.

Chandia, *Chamar*, has left a wife and daughter who await his return or news. The wife in question lost her father and a brother from famine in 1878: so her lot has been cast in hard lines. An old woman living on by herself has three children in one of the colonies, who went off together, and would doubtless send her money if duly instructed.

Had been told that there was a returned emigrant here, but he proved to be a reminiscence of the mutiny, a *Brahmin*, who had then been sent to the Andamans for some crime, and had served his time, bringing back money.

In the evening rode to Parehtah and Moharia Khurd. Many people had emigrated, but I learnt nothing of particular interest, as those who had families seem to have taken them. An exception was Badlu, *Kori,* who emigrated in 1870-71, and who is still expected by a wife and children.

Has it never occurred to any one connected with emigration that the death of every emigrant should be notified to his family? I was assured here, as elsewhere, that numbers of people would emigrate if a system of correspondence or communication could be maintained.

March 20th – Moved camp to Mohanlalganj.

Visited the carbonate of soda manufactory in the centre of the usary plain near Kajauli – a trade capable of great extension and apparently hampered very much under the salt laws.

Across the Koraila jhil, ordinarily three miles in circumference, but now perfectly dry and full of fine crops.

To Hulas Khera, where I expected to find the *Pasi* about whom, as a returned emigrant, I had heard so much. Went to the house of Chandi Singh, the *lambardar,* a wise old *Thakur* with a great local reputation as a medicine man. I found a *Mahajan* there who had come all the way from Lucknow to consult Chandi.

Chandi Singh did not think that recruiters visiting villages would be interfered with. "Why should they," said he, "when they are servants of the Government? but he opined that the villagers generally would be *khafa* with them for taking away relatives to 'no one knew where.' It was very hard on the relatives left getting no news; if news could be got, people would be satisfied and would go more freely."

The *Pasi* returned emigrant had after all gone away to another village. From the *chaukidar,* whose sister the *Pasi* in question had originally married, I learnt that the man emigrated 18 or 20 years ago, and had returned lately, bringing back another wife and three children, he himself being paralysed on one side. His first wife and son rejoined him. Then came quarrels about caste, the brethren insisting on three or four dinners, while the emigrant would only agree to give one. Eventually he turned his first wife out of doors, keeping the few cooking vessels which she had with her, and went off to another village. Evidently emigration had improved this man's worldly means, but not his morality.

The *chaukidar* knew of no others having emigrated. Moti, *Kori,* died of hunger, and his son Auseri disappeared (had emigrated). Samadhan, *Dhobi*, fell sick in 1876, and, when unable to do more than crawl, could get no food and died.

Umrao,[8] his son, disappeared (emigrated to Natal), leaving a wife with son and daughter, a brother and other relatives. To these people to hear that I could say where the man had gone was like a revelation.

Ramzan Ali, a fine old Musalman of Kajauli, came to my tents at midday to enquire whether I could obtain news for him of his son Shere Ali, who emigrated in 1877, leaving a girl to whom he was betrothed and who is still unmarried. The old man said that all he cared for in life was to see or hear of this son again, and I promised to write for him.

N.B. – Have since found that Shere Ali embarked for Grenada in the *Hermione* in December, 1877, and have written to him.

Left for Lucknow in the afternoon, and found a letter from Dr Grant informing me of the arrival of the *Sylhet* with returned emigrants from Trinidad, but the letter had been delayed in progress, and it was too late to see the men.

March 21st – Visiting the Lucknow depots in the morning. Near the railway met a large batch of coolies for Natal on their way to Calcutta: they had come from Aligarh and stations thereabout, had rested for a time in Lucknow and would rest at Fyzabad for a day and again at Benares. Through special carriages for coolies would obviate this. The people were straggling about, and could easily have deserted, if so inclined.

First to the Demerara depot. Very dirty. Inspected recruiters' licenses and badges. The vernacular portion of the licenses not filled in. The recruits in depot, principally women, some sadly wanting in clothing.

Visited Ganeshganj depot. Apparently recruiting going on both for Fiji and Natal by the sub-agents in partnership. Depot more roomy and cleaner than the first visited. A woman here, who, from her officiousness I should guess, does some recruiting.[9] A few coolies here who were out of condition and were resting until fit for labour.

Passed Natal depot No. 3. Small and dirty. No coolies, the batch I met having just left this place.

Depot in Nayagaon. A spacious enclosure with houses all round and a large *Baradari* in the centre, good well, and separate latrine accommodation for the sexes; rather dirty.

A large number of coolies collected for Fiji. There were in this depot nine fine young men from one village in Gonda, who told me that seven men had emigrated from the same village some few years back, of whom three men and one woman had returned, bringing so much money that the speakers were tempted to try their luck also. The three men alluded to had soon again emigrated, disgusted with the cupidity of their fellow villagers.

These men seemed to be in high spirits, looking forward to their new life. They all admitted to having families at home, but considered them perfectly safe with their caste brethren, and remarked that it was the custom of the country to go forth in this way, leaving families behind.

Of the original seven it was reported that three had permanently settled in Demerara. It struck me that the men before me thought Fiji close to Demerara, so I explained the position.

At the Aminabad depot a complaint was made of rent being due for about a year from the Demerara Sub-Agent.

The emigrants above alluded to as returning to Gonda are stated to have said that they never could remit money.

No rule in these depots as to the amount of food given, but care is evidently taken to keep the people well. Sometimes, though seldom, they get cash, if preferring it. The *chulas* show that the coolies are allowed to cook for themselves.

It must not be forgotten, when the time comes for depots to be supervised by Magistrates and Civil Surgeons, that the system of the coolies cooking, each with their own *chula,* should not be interfered with, otherwise officers will be apt to order *chulas* to be cleared out on the score of untidiness and want of uniformity. *Chulas* are certainly not insanitary. With reference to Lucknow registration, I may note that I happened in February last to attach, as Judge of the Small Cause Court, the property of a Sub-Agent who had been dismissed a year or so ago. Amongst other things was a daily expenditure account-book, in which I found entries of payments to various *kutcherry* clerks, evidently as bribes. There were, however, similar entries as paid to the Emigration Agent's Bengali Inspector, when the latter visited Lucknow.

22nd March – At Cawnpore, where I met the Collector and arranged for an inspection of the register. Also met Mr Buck, Mr Benett and Mr Fuller.

23rd March – Had a talk with Mr Buck on matters emigrational and saw letter to Mr Rivers Thomson about the resolution to be issued to the North-Western Provinces.

Examined the registers; found all sorts of eccentric spelling in names of places and people. The following are a few specimens of the spelling of the names of North-Western Provinces and Oudh districts:

Fanltap's, Unan, Fuchpore, Shajahpur (Shahjahanpur?), Aleegudh (Aligarh?); others quite unintelligible; Sandila put down as in Lucknow instead of Hardoi. It seems the practice here to make the recruiters bring the copies of the registers, which are sent to Calcutta, written out first in the *bazaar*. The Magistrate then signs them, and they are afterwards copied into the book register, which latter the Magistrate does not sign, nor is the certificate required in circular affixed. Clerk gets a fee of 2 *annas* per coolie.

24th March – Visited the Cawnpore depots accompanied by a police officer.

1. For Natal and Demerara on the Thandi Sarak. The Sub-Agent here is a *Brahmin* widow, who has been thus employed for 18 years. She appoints an agent by power-of-attorney and works through him. Her husband when alive was also a Sub-Agent.

Her present manager, Kullu, holds a license, and she employs several licensed recruiters at Rs. 8 each per mensem, also a writer at Rs. 8 per mensem.

Coolies receive food, not cash, and cook for themselves. If ill or thin, are kept till fit for work. It is against the interests of the recruiter to starve a man.

Courtyard dirty; one well and latrine. A good airy upper story. Women and men occupy separate parts of the house, but have only one latrine in common.

Great complaints were about the *Kotwal,* and the Cawnpore rule, which requires that every coolie shall be taken to the police station and there interrogated before going to the depot. The police officers, it is said, abuse the coolies and emigration, and in consequence many desert. The only coolies in depot were:

1. A *Chamar* woman residing formerly in the Unao district; lost her husband two months ago and wandered to Cawnpore; could not earn a living at home.
2. A lad from Aligarh.
3. A *Brahmin* from Etawah.

Both of the latter had wandered down in search of work and were seedy, for which reason they had not been sent on with the last batch. Both gave me the impression of life-weary men who had wandered far, ill-fed and unable from weakness to earn sufficient wherewith properly to recruit their strength. For such men to find food supplied gratis, and perfect rest for perhaps six months and good wages to follow, must surely seem a wonderful boon.

A returned emigrant lives opposite this depot. The people said that he brought back Rs. 800 or 900 a year ago and gambled it all away. I sent for him, but he was out somewhere.

Sub-Agent receives Rs. 22 per man and Rs. 33 per woman; also a bonus at the end of the season of Re. 1 per individual over 100. 2nd depot (close by 1st), Trinidad and Fiji. Sub-Agent Baldeo, *Brahmin*, (licensed), a brother of Munshi Jasodha and seemingly a most respectable quiet man.

Two licensed recruiters in depot, who both frequently travel to Calcutta with coolies. Have no complaints to make against the Railway police and are on friendly terms with those at Howrah. If ever they tip them, it is to help in getting a dinghy or for some similar service.

This is easily understood, as one of them was a Police *sepoy* formerly in Calcutta. Both respectable intelligent men, Muhammadans, residents of the Unao district.

This depot was much cleaner than No. 1 and in fair order. Only one coolie present, a *Lodh* of the Cawnpore district. He said that he had left a betrothed whom he would gladly have taken with him, only her parents would not give their consent. Opined that if he did not return after 4 or 5 years she would probably marry some one else. No writer kept here. Any Babu in the *bazaar* employed. Nothing to pay at *kutcherry* besides the registration fee, which has lately (they say) been reduced to Re. 1.

No. 3 depot, also near No. 1, managed by Ahmad Shah (unlicensed) for Ewaz Ali, Sub-Agent of Trinidad. One of the recruiters here apparently acting on a Demerara license. Depot airy and fairly clean. One coolie present, a woman from the Sultanpur district, who has been detained here for a whole month while enquiries are being made, through the police, as to whether she has a husband; says that she has no one dependent on her; looks as if she had been on the town.

No. 4 depot, Colonelganj, a much cleaner and more spacious depot than any of the others. Ahmed Khan (licensed) manages it for Mozuffer Ali, Sub-Agent for Demerara and Natal. Several recruiters here, all respectable-looking men enough and residents either of Lucknow or Cawnpore. Great complaints about the police. A number of coolies here for Natal. One woman with two children, who has already been to Calcutta once and was rejected on account of ill health, says she is now quite well and is anxious to go again.

No. 5 depot, Natal, Sub-Agent Birbal; writes his own accounts, but also keeps a writer. Nabi Buksh, a smart-looking man and a recruiter in the depot, gets Rs. 10 a month; was formerly a *khidmatgar*, very quick and intelligent. Complained bitterly about the police here and at Agra, where he had lately been, but ascribed some cases in which certain recruiters had been prosecuted by the Agra police to 'want of experience.' Told an amusing story how a *Thakur* had answered a Magistrate. The latter said, 'You will have to travel 3,000 kos.' 'That's nothing,' said the *Thakur;* 'I will go 6,000.' 'The ship will go up and down like that' (showing with his hands.) 'Then I will go like that', replied the *Thakur,* moving his hands the other way. 'You will lose caste,' said the Magistrate; 'you may be forced to do work you object to.' 'Not so long,' said the *Thakur*, 'as the British Raj has any power:' whereupon he was registered. The recruiter declared that this had actually occurred only lately and gave names, but it is probably a stock story. Birbal has recruiters stationed at Unao and Farukhabad, Agra and Muttra and Delhi. Curiously enough, the only two coolies here were both returned emigrants. One Din Muhammad returned from Demerara 18 months ago, after an absence of 15 years; took his wife out with him and brought her back. Had money, but his wife's illness and death six months ago cost him a great deal. Was now going to try his luck in Natal, though he would rather go to Demerara, if only the season were open.

Spoke with intense scorn of Hindustan, as being unfit to live in after Demerara. No short-commons there, no famine. I drew him out by suggesting that it was very cold, that they could not get fish, and so on, which elicited from him lavish praise of everything and every one connected with Demerara as compared with Hindustan. With him was his son, a boy of 5 or 6, and particularly bright and intelligent. The child had returned from Demerara speaking English, but could now only say a few words, which however he seemed very pleased to have an opportunity of using. (2) Balmukand, a *Thakur* from Bhartpur, returned from Jamaica six months ago, after an absence of only five or six years, having, so he said, got a passage through the favour of his master. Had left a wife and children before and was leaving them again. Laughed at the idea of taking them with him.

Was very happy in Jamaica, where he had a horse and some cattle, but met with losses, and on the way home coming up-country was robbed in the train, while asleep, by another returning emigrant, a Musalman, who had always been his great friend.

These men had nothing to say against their treatment on the sea journey either going or returning, and seemed to dwell with pleasure on the liberal allowance of food on shipboard. The voyage however was tedious, and they seemed comforted to know that the voyage to Natal was so much shorter.

They concurred in saying that letters were torn up by the Negro postmen and that letter-writing was discouraged, also that the rates of postage and rates for remittance were prohibitory. A paper went round once a year, in which coolies entered the sums they wished to remit.

A grievance was the having to pay for the return passage of children who had gone out free or had been born in the colony.

A difficulty with these men was to make them speak in Hindustani instead of the broken English, of which they seemed, as all returned coolies do, extremely proud; though their patois is somewhat interlarded with expressions common in use amongst sailors' parrots.

25th March – Depot large and fairly-well arranged, a congerie of huts in a compound giving families and women separate rooms.

This is really the depot for the French Colonies, but recruiting for the latter being closed for the season, it is temporarily occupied by coolies for Natal under Ahmad Khan (licensed). A number of coolies were ready to start; some had left families in charge of relatives. One woman had had her nose bitten off and had no desire to remain with her husband.

The French Sub-Agent (Mr Moses) was away, but a very intelligent man was in charge, Rahim Husain, a Turk from Bagdad (licensed).

Complaints again about the Agra and Cawnpore police and about registration as conducted by a Native Magistrate at Rae Bareli.

26th March – Returned to Lucknow, and by post received formal complaints against the way of conducting registration at Rae Bareli and Etawah. At the latter place it was said that for three days running the recruiter had been told at *kutcherry* to 'come again,' and then that two holidays had supervened.

Visited the depots in the morning and found a recruiter who had come from Etawah to report. Interviewed the Babu, who writes for the depot about his work.

Budhu Khan, a man whom I had left at Mohanlalganj with list of names from the registers, with directions to enquire about families in villages where I was unable to go, brought in reports signed by *patwaris* or *lambardars* of each village. They contained the usual tale of numbers having left, but no news. One boy was found tending cattle who had lost both his parents in some colony and had been sent back to his home. He is still only 12 years of age. Ramdin, *Ahir*, been absent 14 years; wife still in village and unmarried.

Shewla and Chakna, *Pasis*, brothers, left wives and families. A son of Shewla's has remained and maintained the whole family. Chakna's wife lives with her parents.

Ajudhia, *Kurmi,* of Nagraon left his wife and children 15 years ago and went to Mauritius. He has sent two remittances, one of which had been received, but the other for Rs. 50 has not come to hand. A brother to whom the letter was sent came along with Babu Khan and showed me the letter, a most commonplace affair for an absentee of 15 years. His only enquiry was as to how the rice crops of a certain field were this year.

Bhagoleh, *Gujur*, left 15 or 16 years ago; wife and son still in village.

Total 37 people traced, but news and remittance from one only.

Sanaullah, recruiter from Shahjahanpur, came to see me. Says that his father was a *zamindar* in Bara Banki. Has recruited for 13 or 14 years. Complains that the Deputy Collector refuses to register any one save residents of the district. Also that he tells the coolies that they will become *be din.*

Cawnpore, which used to be a good district, has much fallen off.

Hyder Hussein, who lately worked for Demerara and Natal, came.

Says that the rent of the Natal depot complained of as in arrears is due from Mozuffer Ali. Also the pay for six months of a recruiter (who also complained to me this morning).

Talked of the capabilities of different districts: Umballah, Delhi, and Rohilkhand for men only, while Muttra is a particularly good district for women, who crowd there as widows on pilgrimage.

Agra and Muttra are also good districts as being adjacent to native states, the inhabitants of which are very hard up as compared to our territories.

Cawnpore and Colonelgunge are great *Nakas,* where many coolies can be got.

Women very plentiful in Ghazipur, Azamgarh, and thereabouts; Rae Bareli good, especially for women, but great opposition from the Native Deputy Magistrate.

Recruiters go out on the roads with three or four *chaprasis* and send men on to the depot, as recruited, by a *chaprasi.*

They go amongst the villages in some districts. Formerly interference with recruiters was forbidden from time to time by *munadi* or by beat of drum through the common crier.

A *Kahar* woman who returned not long ago from some colony with 3 to 4,000 *rupees* and a quantity of jewelry has again emigrated, taking along with her some 19 other women.

Another female emigrant recently returned to reside in Lucknow brings some Rs. 3,000 in cash and a quantity of ornaments.

Police interference is everywhere the most serious drawback to successful recruiting. Interviewed another recruiter by name Sher Khan, who has held a license without fault for 22 years. His father was a *sepoy* in the King of Oudh's service. Another, Ram Charan, *Bania,* resident of Fyzabad, a young respectable-looking man, who has so far done no other work.

At the depot this morning I found a recruiter of 20 years' service who was formerly a *darwan* in Calcutta (Madar Baksh by name). He had just brought three men registered at Etawah: (1) a *Thakur* from Etah, (2) a *Thakur* from Etawah, (3) a Musalman from Bhartpur.

All three knew perfectly well what they were about and were free from any sort of shyness. One had been ill for two or three days, but had been dosed and was now recovering.

In another of the depots a man, in reply to my query as to why he did not take his wife with him replied that his wife's parents prevented her from accompanying him.

27th – Rae Bareli. Went with Deputy Commissioner to look at the depot, but found it had been closed for some time past.

The Deputy Commissioner, who had lately come, could give me no information, but gave me every assistance. Examined the register and found that in this district, residents of which are recruited in hundreds in other districts, not a single recruit had been registered for over a year.

The register was in fairly correct order, but no office copies are kept of monthly returns A and B. Clerk has never drawn fees.

Found, as stated in complaints, that the native Extra Assistant only registers those belonging to the district, and also only low castes, and no females. As only those coolies were entered who had passed, I could not tell how many had been rejected.

In 1868, one batch alone of 30 (the first) was composed as follows:

By District	Male	Female
Rae Bareli	11	7
Azamgarh	3	4
Sultanpur	2	1
Partabgarh	1	-
Unao	1	-
	18	12
	30	

By caste

Brahmins and Thakurs	3	2
Musalmans	2	1
Ahirs and Garariyas	4	1
Low castes	9	8
	18	12
		30

This shows the commencement of recruiting under fair auspices: a large proportion of women, a good admixture of castes, and men from surrounding districts as well as from Rae Bareli.

In 1879, before the Extra Assistant Commissioner, only two coolies were registered.

In 1880, none.

In 1881, January to March, 22 registered, all from Rae Bareli, and only one female.

In fact, on the figures of the last four years, Rae Bareli has the fewest registrations of any district in the North-Western Provinces and Oudh where recruiting has been opened, though, as has been remarked, its people emigrate freely on going to other districts.

The head clerk here, whom I knew well as an old *Munsarim* of mine, said that there was practically very little deception practised now, and that the country-people were well able to take care of themselves.

The Deputy Commissioner, before I left, promised to take the registration, and either do it himself or give it to a European officer. (No complaints since 25th May, 1882).

28th – At Lucknow. Wrote to Emigration Agent for Demerara, through whom complaints had been received; also to Collectors of the districts towards which I shall proceed. Interviewed the *munshi* of the Trinidad depot.

29th – Left for Fyzabad and arrived there in the p. m.

Examined registers, which were brought to me by the clerk who keeps them, and keeps them intelligently, being apparently at the trouble to make himself well acquainted with emigration affairs. Said that people were fully alive in this district to the advantages of emigration, being educated thereto by the large sums remitted through the treasury and by the numbers who have lately returned.

Those who return frequently re-emigrate with their families, taking fellow villagers along with them, of which he pointed out to me in the register the following instances:

On the 21st March, 1882, the last entries which had been made previous to my arrival were those of nine men of several different villages of the district who were proceeding in a body under the guidance of an old emigrant of Demerara, a *Kumhar*. There were four *Ahirs,* two Musalmans, one *Pasi*, and a *Brahmin* besides the *Kumhar.*

In February 1882, Wazir, a Musalman, re-emigrated, taking with him his wife and two married couples from the same village.

In November 1881, a *Kori* re-emigrated, accompanied by three *Koris* from the same village.

In July 1881, Surju, *Barhai*, re-emigrated, accompanied by mother, wife, three brothers, one sister and two cousins.

In January 1880, two *Ahirs* from a village in Rae Bareli re-emigrated with their families, a total of four men and five women.

In December 1880, another old emigrant carried back with him nine relatives and friends from the same village.

The Adjudhiya fair is very fruitful in recruits. In one day's entry I found a batch of seven *Chattris* from Ahmadabad (Gujerat) and one *Brahmin* from Poona, evidently time-expired pilgrims.

Families appear in greater numbers in the Fyzabad register than in those I have yet seen. Coolies after staying in depot a short time not unfrequently get permission to go and bring their families.

Most of the recruits appear to have belonged to neighbouring districts or to Fyzabad itself, with a fair number from Nepal.

Interviewed the *Kotwal*, who has been here for some years. Between the police and the emigration officials there is perfect accord. The *Kotwal* acknowledged that whenever any one made a complaint of relatives being abducted, every facility was given for enquiry or search, and the emigration people, on the other hand, say that the police never unduly interfere.

Kotwal does not think that women recruiters would be objectionable, provided always that their characters were good, or rather their conduct. As a matter of fact, women living with recruiters do help to recruit.

During the evening visited depots.

1. Muzaffar Ali's Demerara and Natal. Separate sleeping-places for men and for women. Ample room and airy. More rooms being added. About 30 or 40 coolies in depot, some registered at Muttra and some at Delhi, all resting here on their way down. One man, who was registered at Muttra four months ago, and a woman, who had been registered at Aligarh about the same time, had since contracted fever and been unable to proceed. Both seemed perfectly comfortable and satisfied, and said they had received all they wanted and medicine. The man was nearly fit to proceed, but the woman seemed to be in a consumption.

Talked with the coolies for some time and found them anything but shy.

2. Mr Isaac's depot for Trinidad and Fiji. Mr Isaac, a most respectable and intelligent man, a Jew of either Arabic or Syrian extraction, has been employed in the department for some 15 or 16 years.

Has two separate depots some distance apart, one for single men and the other for married people and single women. Both depots large and commodious and kept clean. Keeps no sort of guard over the depot of single men, but allows the coolies to wander in and out just as they like. Finds no great loss from this, though men do occasionally desert owing to the alarming tales they hear from the townspeople, who are said to take every opportunity they can of plying the coolies with reasons for not going. Has over 30 recruiters at work in different districts. Districts differ greatly according to the *hakim-ke-mizaj*. Bahraich Hakim's *mizaj* good and no trouble found. In Gonda, police enquries are instituted in the cases of all women, a *sepoy* going with the woman to her village, and great difficulty in consequence in procuring recruits. Registration in Basti entirely closed owing to the language used towards the coolies by the Deputy.

In the men's depot found a *Lodh* who had been to Jamaica for five years, and falling sick had been given a free return passage and had brought back Rs. 600. Was now going to essay Fiji after staying at home two years. I asked him if he spoke English; 'yas sarr,' he said with the accent of a Christy Minstrel, and took off his *pagri* to make me a bow.

Mr Isaac says that Gonda and Basti furnished many recruits in former years. A recruiter is stationed at Partabgarh (a densely populated district), but has not been very successful.

On to another depot kept by another Syrian Jew named E. Mingey. Plenty of room and separate accommodation for men and women. Mingey is kept going by Isaac, and only carries on in a small way; his coolies seemed comfortable and contented.

30th – Interviewed the sub-agents, Mr Isaac and Shaikh Safdar Ali, brother of the regular sub-agent, Muzaffar Ali, who was away. The general drift of their replies was as follows:

The main *nakas* are Fyzabad, Benares, and Allahabad. There are *nahans*, or pilgrimages for bathing, at all. The overcrowded districts of Gonda, Basti, Gorakhpur, and Sultanpur, send many people to

Fyzabad in search of work. Allahabad has the advantage of Rewah and other Native States.

Great obstruction met with from the 'Deputies,' particularly those of Basti, Shahjahanpur, Rae Bareli, Gorakhpur and Jaunpur. Police interfere at Agra, Cawnpore, Basti, Shahjahanpur and Etawah.

Ghazipur no longer a good district for recruits, as the assamis are so well off there (owing, I suppose, to the opium money spent in the district).

People enlist readily from Bahraich, Gonda, Basti, and Gorakhpur, as the standard of wealth is in those districts very low, while at the same time returned coolies are becoming more numerous.

The recruiters of these sub-agents move freely about the villages and are never interfered with. The good results of this appear in the greater number of families proceeding from these districts.

In the sub-agent's opinion the objections to a man's family going are mainly raised by the wife's relations. Men, however, have lately taken to sending remittances to enable their families to follow them. Within the last year Mr Isaac had received remittances for the families of four emigrants, and has sent on those families to the colony to join their relatives.

The object of a remittance was probably to enable the said families to pay up their liabilities, for which they would otherwise be detained by creditors.

Both Mr Isaac and Safdar Ali highly approve of the idea of entertaining female recruiters, as likely above all things to promote the enlistment of single women of better character than those now obtained. It is admitted that the female relatives of recruiters do already assist to some extent in recruiting.

The Railway police and native Railway officials often cause great annoyance and trouble by telling the coolies lies, with a view to preventing them from emigrating. Mogal Sarai, where the coolies often have to wait for some time, seems to bear a particularly bad reputation in this respect.

The Oudh and Rohilkhand Railway only insist ordinarily on putting eight coolies in a compartment, while the East Indian Railway insist in putting in ten. This is represented as a great hardship with the long journey before the coolies. In view of the large custom given by the Agencies to the East Indian Railway in the transport annually of 10,000 coolies from the North-Western Provinces and Oudh to Calcutta, and the fact that the coolies carry the luggage, while ordinary passengers carry an enormous weight in chattels, the sub-agents plead to be allowed to put eight coolies only in each East Indian Railway compartment.

Also that coolie carriages be 'reserved,' as the outside public are apt to try and frighten coolies when travelling with them.

With regard to registration, the chief complaint is that regarding the use by Magistrate of the words *kala pani*. Says the coolie to himself, when he hears a Magistrate Saheb talking to him of *kala pani:*

Kya! ham ne kya kasur, kiya ke ham ko kala pani sunate hain? Tab bhag jata.

Think that Civil Surgeons might easily examine coolies and register them also. Only it must be done either at a dispensary or at a private residence, and not at the jail.

The sub-agents complain of having no one up-country to whom they can prefer their complaints and seek advice from.

Local enquiries through the police much objected to. No people, however poor, will ever openly say before the whole village that they wish their relatives to emigrate or that they consent to their emigrating. A woman who had left her husband and was recruited was restored to him by order after one of these local enquiries, but she was turned out of doors again and found starving on the road. She is now in the depot and refuses to go back, but looks so young that registration has been refused, and the sub-agent does not know what to do with her.

In Mozuffer Ali's depot this morning I found the same woman whom I had seen in Cawnpore and whose nose bad been bitten off. Her case has been referred to Calcutta, as her fearful disfigurement might be objected to there.

This morning I met Major Maynard, District Superintendent of Police. Major Maynard a few years ago visited Rangoon, Java and the Straits, and was so struck by the advantages of emigration for the surplus population of Oudh that he has in the villages always strongly advocated emigration when he found men idling for want of occupation. Captain Barrow in charge of Encumbered Estates has also always done the same, Fyzabad is peculiarly situated in this way.

There is a very large class of men, chiefly *Thakurs* and *Brahmans*, whose caste prevents them from working in the fields at their homes, but who when away soon learn to do like others. These men formerly filled the ranks of the native army or managed in the Nawabi to live on the village rents. This they cannot now do to the same extent under our system.

Large numbers of them migrate to Rangoon to serve as *Darwans*, &c., paying their own passage and remitting money freely. Hence the idea of emigration has less terrors for this district than for most. Another good point was that, so long as Captain Barrow registered emigrants, he made his *munshi* carefully read to the coolies in the vernacular the statement of 'advantages to coolies emigrating' which every colony prepares and circulates, but which, in most districts, is consigned to the records as so much waste paper.

Both the *Kotwal* and the sub-agents remarked that whether matters in a district went well or ill all depended on the *intizam* and *mizaj* of the district officer; and that where these were good, as had for some time been the case in this district, neither the police nor the emigration officials would be found practising evil.

Talking with Mr Quinn, the Commissioner, he gave it as his opinion that the police are too often guilty of attempting to 'run in' recruiters, though he thinks that the latter class might be improved. Was always careful, as a Magistrate, to keep registration in his own hands. Thinks it absurd to consult the relatives of an adult woman as to whether she may emigrate or not; sees no harm in Magistrate on tour pointing out the advantages of emigration. In fact, has done so himself.

1st April – Arrived at Gonda and conferred with the Deputy Commissioner on emigration matters. Inspected the registers at *kutcherry.*

Register not in accordance with circular and too elaborate. No certificate as required; reasons for rejecting coolies not given. Forms A and B slightly incorrect, and other small details pointed out. Clerk gets a fee of 1 *anna* per head. Fresh register started in proper form and clerk duly instructed. The register shows that of late only residents of Gonda have been accepted, saving the presence of a few widows from other districts. So far the Act had been read to mean that the Magistrate of the district could alone register, which of course would stop all recruiting during the best months by reason of the Magistrate being on tour.

Placed matters on a more satisfactory footing and returned to Fyzabad. The Deputy Commissioner of Gonda informed me that he was obliged to get a recruiter's license cancelled lately on account of the latter trying to force some woman to go with him of whom the registration had been refused.

Deputy Commissioner has 7,000 acres of waste land available for emigrants with capital, and in a healthy part of the district.

2nd April – At Fyzabad, interviewed the *tahsildar* and an Extra Assistant Commissioner. The *tahsildar,* among other matters, said that when collecting revenue, people often said that they were hard up, and that if he might recommend emigration to those in want of work, it would be a good thing.

In Gonda, Basti, and Gorakhpur, the ploughmen are regular bondsmen, and the registering clerk at Gonda asked me whether a *zamindar* might not effectually object to a ploughman being registered from whom the *zaminda*r held a bond.

Some one has remarked that the *zamindars* of these districts seem to spend their time in hunting for fugitive slaves, for the ploughmen are no better.

At Basti, called on the Collector and had a long talk, but the emigration here has for a long time remained in the hands of Deputy Collectors.

Approved of Civil Surgeons generally doing the work, but did not think it would answer with all. Has had no cases against recruiters.

Examined the registers which were brought by the clerk. Clerk receives 2 *annas* per coolie.

Only nine adults registered between January, 1881 and April, 1882. The following figures fully bear out the recruiters' assertion as to opposition:

January 1873 to January 1875. Coolies registered by a European officer 1,070. January 1875 to 1876 = 81, partly registered by a European and partly by a native officer. January 1876 to January 1877 = 19; all registered by a native officer. January 1877 to January 1878 = 184, by a native officer.

January 1878 to January 1879 = 59, partly by a European and partly by a native; January 1879 to January 1880 = 380, partly by a European and partly by a native officer.

January and February 1880 = 67. June to January 1881 = 42. All by the Deputy complained of who commenced in January 1880, and then from January 1881 to April 1882, only 9.

Considering the amount of distress in Basti in 1877 and 1878, the above figures are somewhat curious, for in Fyzabad alone from April, 1877 to September, 1878, there were registered 386 people from the Basti district, and 29 were registered at Lucknow.

Registers kept very neatly, but not according to form, and no certificate. Office copies of A and B neatly kept in a book (manuscript).

Deputy Azmat Ali, who registered from 1877 to 1880, rejected freely for no other reason than that 'the emigrant came to the district to seek a livelihood and was recruited;' as if it was a grievance. A remark in register of 1880: 'The enquiry now ended resulting in the fact that she has been forsaken by her husband on account of her unchastity, now allowed to go.' Another, 'a married woman forsaken by her husband on account of her bad conduct.'

Against another detained is entered – 'A widow under enquiry.' And again – 'The man Ram Kishan has disappeared in the course of the enquiry on certain suspicious points connected with him.'

In former years there were residents of numerous other districts registered here, but latterly the coolies all appear as residents of Basti, giving grounds for the assertion that the residents of other districts are rejected.

The Collector promised to see that all errors and wrong impressions should be corrected.

Pressure of population in Basti said to be ordinarily not great. A large river population who, when the Patna-Bahraich Railway is completed, will be thrown out of employ.

In the registers the coolies for each colony are entered collectively in separate parts of the register, and not the batches consecutively. On monthly form A in Gonda, an abstract is given of the castes of those emigrating, which is shown everywhere might be useful.

At Gorakhpur. Emigration here at a standstill on account of the Passover, the sub-agent being a Jew (Mr Joshua), who was away spending the feast elsewhere. Discussed emigration with the Collector. Recruiting for Assam has lately begun here on a system of free labour, of which the Collector seems doubtful. A large amount out of cultivation since 1878, and rents down to half what they were a few years ago. Labour is never scarce. No difficulties about emigration and no cases, except occasionally parents object to their sons going away. Some time ago there was an enquiry about two women being registered here who, it was believed, had been recruited at Chupra. No results.

Interviewed the Deputy Collector. Chatterdhari Thakur has been in the district some 25 years and conducts registration. Thinks that men may be occasionally deceived, but has had no complaints about it. Has heard that recruiters bring men from other districts, but has never had proof. Thinks female recruiters might be tried. Never saw the local depots. Had never seen a 'notice to emigrants,' and on my showing one he himself suggested that the notice should be read out to each batch of recruits.

Examined books. Register serial No. kept monthly.

Note made on it of Civil Surgeon having passed the coolies.

A very full certificate. Only Re. 1 per coolie levied since January (an error which I corrected both here and at Cawnpore). Clerk receives 2 *annas* per coolie.

Notes from Register:

August 1881 – An agriculturist emigrating, accompanied by two wives.

Recruits mainly for Gorakhpur, but also from Chapra, Azamgarh, and Basti, several from Fyzabad, and a widow from Firozpur.

Forty-seven Nepalese registered between April, 1880 and April, 1882 and 46 residents of Basti for the same period.

From January 1877 to September 1878 no less than 1,726 men were registered, though the district suffered less than Basti, where only 223 were registered for the same period.

Interviewed two recruiters, (1) Benah Tewari, a dissipated and disreputable-looking man; had been a servant of Mr Joshua in trade for seven years and a recruiter for one year. (2) Urjun, *Chamar*, had served for a few months as a *chaprasi* and in taking coolies to Calcutta, and had held license for three years. Quiet and orderly to all appearance.

A third man came, a *chaprasi* of the depot, but whom the others called *Jamadar* who had been for years in the department, and, as I afterwards heard, had once been a recruiter, but had had his license cancelled.

These men have only lately arrived and said that registration was not carried on properly, but on cross-examination I found that they had no sort of grounds for complaints. It was only hearsay.

Bitterly complained of Azamgarh, from whence they had just come. Say that the Collector refuses all men not residents of his district and all good-looking women. Ordinarily on account of the number of returned emigrants in the district (from the Mauritius), Azamgarh is a good district for recruits.

Say that the sub-agencies must have separate depots to prevent quarrelling. One of Mr Joshua's *chaprasis* is said to be a returned emigrant, but I did not see him.

A *Bhat* in this district will re-emigrate to Trinidad so soon as the season opens, and will take with him 30 or 40 people from his neighbourhood.

At Howrah the only persons who annoy them are rival recruiters.

Grain is so cheap now in all these eastern districts that coolies are scarce.

There are several European *zamindars* in this district who will not allow recruiting on their estates, whether the people wish to go or not. A recruit who had come from a village on one of these estates having been recognized in the depot by the servant of a European *zamindar*, the latter succeeded in getting the recruiter's license cancelled; otherwise the recruiters go freely into the villages, particularly on a market day, and get the village crier to proclaim their terms. The police ask to see the license, but interfere no further.

The townpeople here said to be very annoying, taunting the recruiters and their recruits as *mirchis*; telling the coolies that the *sahebs* will grind them in mills for oil, &c. I told them (the recruiters) that their only remedy was direct complaint to the Collector, who remarked to me subsequently that Mr Joshua was an old resident and a member of the volunteers, who might be sure of getting every consideration shown to any complaints he might formulate.

Went in the evening to the depot. An untidy place, small and quite unfit for the purpose.

5th April – A bad day of cholera in the town yesterday; went in the morning with Collector to hospital to make enquiries.

Met the *tahsildar*, who said that the only case he could remember within 10 years against recruiters was where two rival recruiters had a free fight and were fined Rs. 25 each.

I have come to the conclusion already that the line between Government and emigration is not visible to the people generally; even the *tahsildars* look on it as a Government matter, but no harm comes therefrom.

6th April – At Azamgarh. Visited the only depot. A very good depot; clean and roomy with rooms for accommodating women separately, and a female *chaprasi* kept to look after them, who probably does a little recruiting as well. Depot is in an open part of the town; 3 licensed recruiters here; depot established for 6 years, within which time there has been no case against recruiters (so they said).

> (1) Jumarati Pathan has served for 6 years. Formerly kept a shop in Azamgarh. Rather a wild-looking creature.

> (2) Matai, converted Musalman (the female *chaprasi* was also a convert), has held a license three years: a quiet respectable man.

> (3) Ramdin, *Ahir, Jamadar,* respectable to all appearances; was formerly a *chaprasi* in Government employ. Holds a contract for his coolies or rather did, but has got, so he says, irretrievably into debt over the business, as I will explain hereafter. On my way to the

depot I met a well-dressed Musalman, from whom I asked the way, on which he volunteered to show me. I took him into the depot with me and referred the assertions made for his opinion also.

The recruiters vehemently denied that they ever went beyond the limits of their districts to recruit. A great many returned emigrants in the district. To register a few coolies two months ago the recruiters had to follow the Collector out into camp. In the depot were 4 men and women who had been registered at Cawnpore, but no Azamgarh recruits, which shows the sub-agents' difficulties. Recruiters are not interfered with when visiting villages. Relatives, however, prevent people from going. Very loud complaints about the police, who, if a relative complains to them, order a recruit to be turned out of the depot without enquiring as to whether he wishes to emigrate or not; say the relatives pay the police to do this. The man who had accompanied me in has a brother in the police. He made no sort of objection to the accusation, but rather confirmed it. The best way the recruiters think to get families to go is to forbid the relatives from interfering. Many men who now go by themselves would take their families, if their wives' relatives did not prevent their doing so.

The recruiters would like the terms offered to be hung up in each *thana*. The enquiries about females carried on in this district through the police have done much to stop recruiting for the last three years. Women are very plentiful in this district, because they are promptly expelled from home and caste when detected. This is carried to a greater extent than in most districts, and the Collector, when I told him of this, remarked that he had noticed how very few adultery cases ever came into court as compared with his experience in other districts, where the people resort to the courts, while here they evidently prefer the *punchayet*.

Recruiters think that women could only go recruiting if accompanied by a man to help them (I suppose if assaulted).

Subsequently Ramdin came to the bungalow to tell me about his difficulties. About June last, a *Chamar* of the Jaunpur district, who had been to Demerara, brought some 17 men, 22 women and 26 children to be registered along with him for Trinidad, there being no agency for Trinidad at Jaunpur, but only at Azamgarh, The ship not being ready, the recruiter fed these people for several weeks, and on taking them up for registration the whole lot were rejected because they belonged to villages in the Jaunpur district, and the recruiter lost the entire sum spent on their food. Hence his state of indebtedness.

The recruiter said he had subsequently seen the same *Chamar* in Calcutta, and heard that the people were registered, some at Jaunpur and some at Benares, for Demerara, though their original plan was to go to Trinidad.

Another reason for these people flocking to Azamgarh was that they were leaving on account of oppression by some *zamindars,* and they feared that the said *zamindars* had influence enough with the *kutcherry* officials of Jaunpur to stop their going.

Recruiters are too jealous to allow of other recruiters venturing within their bounds. Recruiters in these eastern districts frequent village markets or *bazaars,* fairs, melas, &c., and proclaim by beat of drum through the public crier their business. Police do not interfere if the recruiter is duly provided with *chapras* and license. The recruiters object that a badge is as much a safeguard against illegal recruitment as anything else.

Think that an advance, to be paid at time of embarkation to some person named before the Magistrate, might induce families to emigrate in larger numbers, an increased wage to women when going with husband and children, or a free return passage after, say, 7 years. Family people object to the medical examination of women. Relatives are a great hindrance. Of 15 men, women, and children, taken to the Collector's camp a few weeks ago to a place 15 miles off, 2 married couples were passed and the rest were rejected.

In the p.m. examined the registers at *kucherry* and talked over matters with the Collector.

Register slightly informal and much too small; the space for writing village names, &c., being quite insufficient.

Yet here for the first time I came across a letter from Government of Bengal, to Government of India, circulated in North-Western Provinces as No. 2A of 1866, which (para. 7) runs as follows:

> It will be seen from the correspondence forwarded that several inaccuracies have been discovered in the registers of the Protector's office leading to difficulties in the identification of emigrants and the discovery of their heirs in case of death. It appears to the Lieutenant-Governor that the remedy for this is increased care and accuracy in the original registration of emigrants by the local Magistrates. These officers from their acquaintance with local peculiarities of dialect, and their knowledge of local topography, are in a much better position to record accurately the particulars necessary to the complete identification of each emigrant.

Brave words these; but in this transitory world, and in the absence of any one whose business (like that of an Inspector-General) it is to see that circulars are kept up, an injunction of this nature is soon lost sight of; and it seems also to have escaped the notice of the compiler of the Digest, North-Western Provinces Orders, which has lately been issued.

No lists hung up in *tahsils* here, or in any part of the United Provinces that I could learn.

Book register occasionally not signed. Recruiter has to make out the list in English; the office writer gets 2 *annas* a coolie, and should do all the English work.

Only coolies who are passed, and not those who are rejected, entered in register: consequently it is impossible to test the recruiter's statements of wholesale rejections; but this the Collector in his letter to Government quoted above virtually admits, and curiously also admits that he knows it to be illegal. Collector can only remember one complaint against recruiters, and that was the case of the married women from the Jaunpur district, upon which the Government Circular No. 88 of 1879 was based. Records of the case are with the Jaunpur Magistrate.

Number registered at Azamgarh:

1873	712	1878	376
1874	259	1879	102
1875	125	1880	131
1876	56	1881	51
1877	414		

A curious correspondence here between the Protector of Emigrants, Calcutta, and the Collector, extending from November, 1880 to September, 1881, about one, Ajudhia, *Brahman*. The Protector wrote up to say that the man had died in the Calcutta depot and wished to know who the next-of-kin was, as there was property. On enquiry at the village, the man said to be dead was found alive and well and had just returned from colonies, but it took some time to convince the Protector that such was the case. This illustrates the necessity of some reform in the present system of maintaining an emigrant's identity.

7th April – At Jaunpur; examined registers; there are several streams of traffic which, owing to the bridge over the Gumpti, converge on Jaunpur.

From Fyzabad to Benares, from Lucknow to Benares, and from the trans-Gogra and trans-Gumpti districts and Allahabad. Hence the recruits found here are from all these surrounding districts.

With reference to the story of the *Chamar* who, with his following, was rejected at Azamgarh, I find that, on the 3rd August, there were registered for Demerara from the village of which the Azamgarh recruiter furnished the name of a batch of 11 men, 9 women and 16 children, all *Chamars;* thus bearing out the Azamgarh recruiter's statement in part. The recruiter here also said that this batch formed part of the lot rejected at Azamgarh, and that they all came in of their own accord to be registered. There was no recruiter for Trinidad at Jaunpur, so the people had no choice but to go to Demerara, and they had heard, it seems, of the rest of their party having got registered at Benares for Demerara.

Register according to Circular, but next-of-kin too frequently recorded as nil. Only those coolies who are passed appear in the book. No certificate. No office copies kept of A and B (monthly returns); recruiter has to prepare in English the coolies' certificates. Office writer has never received any fee.

Numbers registered:

1873	282	1878	60
1874	175	1879	43
1875	66	1880	106
1876	28	1881	105
1877	78		

8th April – Visited the only depot along with the Collector. It is a small house in the centre of the *bazaar*, and only fit for a small number. The recruiter said that the Azamgarh 'batch' went to the *sarai*. This man's license had been taken from him on suspicion some weeks ago by the late Officiating Collector. The case appeared to be that a girl was brought up for registration, who appeared to be under age, and an enquiry ordered. It was found that, whatever the girl's age, she had been living as a prostitute in the city for some time. The recruiter was then ordered to produce the girl, but, naturally enough, he had declined to keep her any longer when he found her registration objected to, and she had gone away: wherefore his license was impounded, and he had been unable in consequence to work for some weeks. The present Collector agreed that the impounding for no recorded reason had been arbitrary, and I was afterwards able to inform him that the girl had gone to Benares, and having got herself registered there, had gone to Demerara. It is on this question of age that Magistrates seems to find most fault with recruiters. After all, it is a matter of opinion on which people may often fairly differ, particularly when natives of India are concerned, and it should be left for the medical officer to decide. If he passes the supposed girl or boy, his decision should be final. In any case, as the power of rejecting lies with the Magistrate, the order of rejection should be passed, but the fact of a difference of opinion should not involve the entire stoppage of recruiting operations. The recruiter is a resident of Jaunpur, and in slack times works at his trade of *patwa*; says that he is only paid Rs. 5 a month.

Examined the records of the case before referred to as the one on which the North-Western Provinces' Government Circular regarding the registration of women was based.

The woman was registered with two children on the 21st December, 1878, and sailed for Demerara. She told the registering officer that she had no one to support her.

The husband, who resided in the Azamgarh district, first complained on the 27th March, 1879, and in his subsequent examination before the Magistrate, admitted that there had been a quarrel, and that the woman had left her home to go to Jaunpur. There was therefore neither seduction from home nor recruiting in the Azamgarh district, and removal to the Jaunpur district for registration to escape detection. The husband made no attempt to recover his wife until he heard through one of the same batch of coolies (a resident of Jaunpur) who had been rejected at Calcutta, that his wife emigrated.

On a review of the case, Government held that the husband was alone to blame.

I omitted to note that when at Gorakhpur the recruiters said that recruiting for the Mauritius had been stopped for some time, and that for some reason or other Mauritius had become *badnam* amongst the people. The term *Mirchia* being now a regular word of abuse. Coolies were known to say sometimes, 'send us anywhere but to *Mirch*.'

The Deputy Collector at Gorakhpur also said that three Nepalese returned emigrants lately cashed at the treasury a draft of Rs. 1,200. They said that the only fault that they had to find with the colony from which they returned was that 'Niggers' (sic) were favoured as compared to Indians. He could not say which colony it was, but I have seen a remark in some one of the Colonial Reports, though I cannot now find it, that the coolies complained of the partiality shown towards negroes. I think it must have been in St. Vincent.

9th April – Benares. Visited depots. (1) Mauritius, at Birna Bridge. Sub-Agent, Durga Parshad.

This was the only Mauritius depot that I could find in the North-Western Provinces, the rest being, I believe, in Bengal. A *Babu* from Calcutta (Isan Chandar), Inspector of Depots, happened to be here. Depot very small and unfit, but having a very large garden at the back open to the coolies. A very fine-looking Musalman here, a resident of the Panjab, but who had lately returned from the Andamans. I did not enquire particularly into the crime which had sent him there, and it is to be hoped that in emigrating he really wished to obtain a chance of reforming.

The recruiters complained of great difficulty in getting recruits, owing, they thought, to the terms appearing lower than those for other colonies.

No complaints either against the police or of delay in registration.

1. Depot (lndra-ke-pul) Demerara and Natal. Sub-Agents, Muthra Parshad and Kanhaia Lal.

Have worked as such for about three years. Entertain several recruiters.

Debidin, of 5 years' service; Kundharan of 7 years' service; Mohesh Parshad, 9 years' service; Kasi, of 8 years: mostly residents of Benares. The first two are under suspension for various causes, and the last had his license suspended last year because two coolies failed to pass the medical examination in Calcutta who had passed up here. The medical officer here then said that there must have been false personation before him (recruiters' own story).

Depot is in a large garden with plenty of room, and it was asserted that no guard was kept, which apparently was the case. Found here, as elsewhere, that the vernacular part of the licenses is not filled in, so the police can get no information from examining them. I have since pointed this out to Dr Grant, who has ordered the necessary additions to be made.

2nd depot in Kazipura. Sub-Agent, Mr John Caylor (an Eurasian) on behalf of Mr Jacob Moses of Allahabad.

John Caylor says he does not recruit, and holds a license for Surinam only, recruiting for which colony is not now open. Accommodation fairly sufficient as to space, but very untidy and dirty. Room enough to keep women and men separate. Several coolies here from other districts, all of whom told me that they had been recruited in the city. One recruiter, a *Bania*, who has held a license for 3 or 4 years. This man complained of having to fee so many people in the *kutchery*, from the *Babu* who registered his license to the *chaprasi* who marshalls the coolies in *kutchery*. The police also expect something whenever any enquiries are made through them. Has recruited in other districts, but never had to pay like this before. Gets pay and a contract as well. Has no accounts.

John Caylor used to recruit at Fatehpur. Registration went on well enough then, but has heard since of a row there in connection with the recruiters of some other agency about money deposited by a coolie.

In the afternoon interviewed Muthra Parshad and his brother, who say that they employ some 8 recruiters. Say also that Mauritius is unpopular, and can give no reason, as amongst recruiters themselves Mauritius is considered to be the best of the colonies. Azamgarh and Jaunpur good districts for coolies on account of the returned men. Have only heard of a few letters at any time arriving from the colonies. Some time ago a batch of 20 people connected with each other went in a body. One of them was rejected in Calcutta, and a few days ago this man came to the depot to complain that a letter which had arrived for him from the colonies had been taken by his *zamindar* who would not give it up.

About Benares the recruiters do not go into the villages for fear of the *zamindars*, but frequent the highways and attend fairs.

Think that the experiment of female recruiters might be tried, but are not sanguine of success.

Do not complain of the police, but are under the cantonment police; and say the other depot where I found complaints, is under the city police.

There is a system of sub-contract, I now find, between the sub-agent and the recruiter. Hitherto all mention of sub-contract has been avoided.

More families could be induced to go if it were safe for the recruiters to visit the villages and if families could get advances.

Returned emigrants, as a rule, much too cheeky to make good recruiters.

Recruiters have to get the whole of the certificates for the coolies made out before going to a *kutchery*.

With the sub-agents was another recruiter, a young man who had been a domestic servant before, and had held a license for two months.

10th April – Mr Emerson (Eurasian), Sub-Agent for Demerara and Natal at Allahabad and Jabbalpur, came to see me and explain his greivances, which amounted to this:

> 1. That the multiplication of sub-agencies and recruiters leads to much jealousy, rivalry, and quarrelling.
>
> 2. That Magistrates use the words *Kalapani*.
>
> 3. That the townspeople chaff the coolies.
>
> 4. That the character of the sub-agent and recruiters up-country is so often bad.

Keeps no *bandish* at his depot. Allows each coolie daily 1 1/2 *annas*, giving them as well tobacco, wood and oil. Keeps for their use a barber and a *dhobi*.

Also keeps a writer and employs three recruiters at Allahabad and three at Jabbalpur.

Of the Jabbalpur recruiters, one knows English. Does not give the recruiters sub-contracts, but pays them each Rs. 7 a month. The *challandar*, who goes to Calcutta, gets but 4 *annas* a day extra.

Each Demerara sub-agent has to maintain a *darwan* in the Calcutta depot to look after his particular coolies, as the office *Baboos* there say that each sub-agent must be responsible for his own coolies until embarkation.

(Since then I have heard that in consequence of some quarrel between these independent *darwans*, the Agent for Demerara has turned them all out and has put in men of his own.)

Sees no reason why returned emigrants should not make good recruiters.

Has a recruiter at Mirzapur, and so far has encountered no difficulty. The same at Etawah.

Referred to the *jamadar* at Gorakhpur as a case in point of an offending recruiter being still employed; said that there were other dismissed recruiters still working on, some of them under changed names.

Has tried recruiting in villages, but has not found it answer. The villagers say that 'so long as they have plenty of work in the fields at home, why should they go?' And it is only when field work fails that the villagers go wandering to the towns for work. So long as they can earn half an *anna* a day at home they refuse to emigrate.

The *Sadha Bharats* of Benares, five in number, where food and clothes are given free at certain hours daily, attract the poor and recruiters also. *Sarais* and railway stations are also good places wherein to find recruits.

Wishes that agents would visit the up-country depots once in three months, or even six months.

Complains about the Railway, that even when a compartment is filled up with a full complement of 10 coolies and secured at the main station as 'reserved,' other passengers are forced in at intermediate stations. Has a license. Finds it difficult to get the right number of women, but thinks that female recruiters would not answer, as being more untruthful than the men.

Examined registers and abstracted the numbers for 1880-81 by districts.

Registers very slovenly kept in unbound books with brown paper covers, and the treasury receipts for fees pasted in against each batch of coolies, a most unnecessary and confusing proceeding.

Column of 'number' in register runs any how. One series from May 1880, to February 1881; another from March, and in a third from July 1881, up to date. Book not signed by Magistrate, and no certificate. Column of occupation left out, and a column added not in form, in which Magistrate puts his initials against each name.

All coolies brought up are entered, and those not passed are erased without remark.

Sometimes the column of 'next-of-kin' is omitted, and the name of the recruiter appears in its place, while in other places it is the reverse.

Against one coolie appeared the entry 'destroyed.' As the clerk had not come with the books, I could get no explanation.

Searched for the Jaunpur *Chamars*, and found that 8 men, 14 women and 15 children were registered from the villages aforementioned in Jaunpur. It was said here that Jagru had registered some more of the party at Ghazipur, but I found a Jagru, *Chamar*, in the same month (August) from Azamgarh with a good many *Chamars* from that district also.

A case of careless entry here was a district written as 'Nauranga.'

In the afternoon Muthra Parshad again came, accompanied by Debi Parshad, one of his recruiters, and also three returned coolies.

Debi Parshad said that his license had been suspended after 5 years' service, because a *Chamar* woman, who in Benares said she had no next-of-kin, said in Calcutta that she had a husband at Benares, while at Calcutta she had another husband, and also a father and mother.

Another recruiter, Deoki Rahar, was formerly bearer to some Executive Engineer, with whom the sub-agent worked as *Munshi;* has had a license 3 years.

The returned coolies were: (1) Din Muhammad, lately returned from Trinidad after an absence of 13 years; (2) Ganga Ram Dhobi also returned with the latter from Trinidad after 13 years' absence; (3) Rattan Lal Kait, returned from Trinidad 18 months or so ago after 12 years' absence.

None of these men seem to have brought back much money, still they had nothing but good to say of Trinidad, and had heard that Demerara was better still; all talked English after a fashion and were very proud of it.

Said that Arjun Singh, a coolie originally from Ghazipur, had amassed wealth, and having started a sugarcane plantation had begun to import coolies. The *sahebs* however grew jealous and combined to spoil the sale of his sugar in London, by which he was ruined.

Related marvellous tales of the snakes of Trinidad and of the storms round the Cape. Sometimes the coolies cry from fright. Well satisfied with the treatment on boardship, especially with the food, but complained of the *lascars* occasionally bullying them. Hindustan, a country of thieves and liars, while in Trinidad every one is honest and tells the truth. Used to mob the planters if the latter did not behave fairly about wages. Magistrates very just, and do not favour Creoles more than Indians (Creoles pronounced kirwal). No obstacle to letter-writing beyond the rates of postage.

Ganga Ram said that he was robbed of his savings in the train on the way up from Calcutta.

Rattan Lal was going to set up as a recruiter.

Found in the register as entered on 11th October, 1877, for Jamaica, a number of men from Lucknow and other Oudh districts, some of whose names I remembered amongst those of whom I had enquired when in camp; and I subsequently found that a large number of recruits who were registered at Lucknow on the 8th October for Trinidad were again registered at Benares as noted above. There was no concealment of the fact, for the addresses were all given correctly. Again, man registered on 11th October at Benares for Jamaica appears again in the Lucknow register for British Guiana on 24th October. Doubtless he had either deserted and again re-enlisted or had been rejected by the medical inspector.

More singular still, was the registration at Benares on the 8th July, 1878, 140 coolies, all from Oudh for Trinidad, and again at Lucknow nearly the whole of the same batch registered at Lucknow for Natal on 4th May, 1878.

The years 1877 and 1878, being years of scarcity in the North-Western Provinces and Oudh, recruits crowded in such numbers that possibly batches were ready up-country when there were no ships to carry them to the colony for which originally enlisted, while ships for other colonies might be lying empty. Still, the idea of sub-agents up-country transferring coolies to each other is too suggestive of cattle traffic to be pleasant, and transfers after registration has once been effected should only be allowed in Calcutta under the supervision of the Protector.

11th April – Allahabad.

I travelled for the short distance from Benares to Mogal Sarai with an Eurasian Inspector of Post Offices. Without knowing who I was, my companion entertained me with an account of how the police at the riverside station worked the pilgrims by sending men amongst them.

A man so sent would select a well-to-do pilgrim, and pushing up against him suddenly complaining loudly of having been assaulted. Down came the police to the rescue, and the pilgrim was eventually glad to be let off being kept in custody for the imaginary assault by paying something as 'compensation.'

Hearing this story, recalled to mind the complaints of the Fyzabad sub-agents of the police at this particular place.

Visited the depots.

1. Natal and Demerara. Sub-Agent Mr Moses, who was away for the Passover.

Situated in Ghetto Lal-ke-Theta, a very large enclosure similar to a *sarai*. The depot occupied a range of buildings along one side, and the coolies were free to come and go. One was away bathing in the Ganges. Separate room for women. Three recruiters present.

1. Rahamat Ali says that his family originally held land in Ghazipur. Has worked for 18 years. Seems a respectable and intelligent man. Was one of those who were convicted in the great Allahabad case, but who were released by the Sessions Judge on appeal.

I viewed the site of that historic case, and I wish that some one of the Magistrates, Sessions Judge, Commissioner and High Court Judges, who took so much trouble to write minutes had only seen the place with their own eyes before passing judgment.

2. Siobhan, has served for over 12 years. Formerly kept a shop in Benares.

3. Lalla, a resident of Allahabad, served as depot *chaprasi* for 10 years, and held a license for Trinidad, for three years, but lately quarreled with his master, Jahangir Khan, Sub-Agent for Trinidad who won't pay him some money due, and has come here. Says he only does *chaprasi's* work, while Jahangir Khan says that Lela has been taking coolies to this depot; for some time past, though holding a Trinidad license, because in the first place Lela owes him money, and in the second that the Demerara commission is higher than that given by Trinidad.

Each recruiter they say has two *chaprasis* to help him when recruiting, and the sub-agent maintains two to take *challans*. They are paid Rs. 4 and Rs. 5 apiece, with 2 *annas* and 4 *annas* a day for food when travelling.

Recruiters all work on contract, receiving half of what the sub-agents get, but they are evidently poor.

Police oppress very much. No present complaint against registration, but it is a question of the *sahebs' mizaj*.[10]

Say they go about amongst the villages, and that *zamindars* do not interfere.

There were 7 men and 4 women here. All seemed to be quite clear as to their destination, and to be contented and happy.

One of the recruiters keeps his coolies in a separate house some little distance off, this is to prevent quarrels; but, as the sub-agent only takes delivery at the railway station, he evidently exercises little or no control.

Rations are given, it is said, because coolies when receiving cash will not feed themselves properly.

A *Thakur* of Ballarpur re-emigrated 3 years ago, taking with him 30 others, 8 or 10 of whom were *Thakurs* who had sold land and groves,

Kalwa, *Chamar*, returned from Surinam last year and gave a good account of it; re-emigrated to Trinidad, taking 20 men with him.

Went on to the depot of Jehangir Khan. Small but neat. A *chaprasi* seated at the door. Recruiters out at work. Say that there is no *bandish*, and while I was there a coolie came in who had been out in the *bazaar* to buy some *ghi* for the others. This man, however, was rather an exceptional case. He had evidently been ill for some time and had been here for some 6 months, while he admitted having previously been in the Demerara depot for 6 months trying to get fat, but unsuccessfully. He loudly expressed his readiness to go to any part of the known world. The men in depot were for Fiji. One of them (a *Brahman*) said he belonged to Rewah. Had been on a pilgrimage to Ajudhiya, but got ill there (apparently from cholera) and had been unfit for work for some time. Had a wife and children at home, but was fixed in his determination to emigrate.

Interrogated all the rest as to their knowledge of what they were about. One only, a *Brahman*, seemed a little nervous, but said he was ready to go.

Called on the Collector and on Mr Benson, who conducts the registration very carefully. The latter showed me a register which he keeps of recruiters, in which are noted all changes and all charges brought against the men – a very useful idea.

12th April – Jehangir Khan, Sub-Agent, came to see me. Is a native of Delhi. Was first a *chaprasi*, then a recruiter, and has now been a sub-agent for three years. Says that the capricious way in which rejections are made in Calcutta make it a very uncertain business, and that he is heavily in debt. Coolies who are passed by medical officers up-country are rejected by the medical officers in Calcutta, and the entire cost of the coolies falls on the sub-agent. If a coolie dies before embarkation, only half the contract rate is paid to the sub-agent.

Was once in trouble accused of kidnapping two women, but the case was dismissed and the women went off as coolies to Assam.

Complains of the police, but at the same time admits that a great deal of police interference is brought about by the sub-agencies themselves, who quarrel and compete and set the police on against each other. This is brought about very much by the different rates of commission existing. Trinidad is the lowest, then comes Demerara, French and Surinam.

All sub-agents give contracts to recruiters. For instance, from Allahabad to Calcutta the Trinidad Agency allows the sub-agent Rs. 18 for a man and Rs. 28 for a woman. Rs. 8-13 is the railway fare, and *bhishtis* and sweepers, &c., on the line get small tips; this is to ensure the comfort of coolies, and to keep them together. This with food brings up the cost to Rs. 10 per head, while for his sub-contract the recruiter gets Rs. 6 for a man and for a woman Rs. 7 or 8, for which the recruiter finds everything up to the railway station. According to this there is not much profit on the rate of men, especially if rejections be numerous. The agency pays for licenses, also all expenses if detained in depot over one month. Has been here 3 years, while Mr Jacob has been 2 years. Says that he owes Rs. 4,000. All recruiters get advances. Lala owes him Rs. 50. Admits having tried to get a Fiji license for Lala since the latter deserted. Mr Jacob has ruined him by offering higher commission. Does not think that two different sub-agencies should be allowed to work in the same station.

This sentiment I also heard at Benares, where Muthra Parshad bitterly complained of Mr Jacob setting up a rival depot for Natal (the one in charge of John Caylor). Thinks that no married women ever offer themselves for registration who have not gone wrong, unless they be widows.

None of the recruiters here think that female recruiters would answer. Say that a female recruiter who was formerly employed at Gaya came to grief.

Jehangir declares that one of Jacob's recruiters has also got a license for Assam, and that if there is any difficulty about getting a recruit passed here for Demerara, he or she is sent off to Arrah to be registered there for Assam.

Cannot name any returned coolie. Has evidently no sort of conception himself as to how the various colonies are situated geographically.

Some *talukdars* also came to see me. Their only idea about coolies was that they were required for settling waste lands.

Examined registers. The Assistant Magistrates countersign licenses here, but it can only legally be done by the Magistrate of the district.

Register in book form with printed headings, the only one I have seen yet of the kind: but the size is rather small for writing names in full.

Care not taken in writing the names. Billah for instance, which is really intended Belah, as Partabgarh is sometimes called. Against another is written Oudh for district, and Oudh for the *pargana*.

Serial number follows no system:

Emigrants from 1st April, 1877 to 1st April, 1878=452, while from 1st April, 1878, to 1st April, 1879=903.

13th – Jehangir and Rahmat both came to-day. Jehangir gave me a copy of a recruiter's agreement. Says he has tried fixed salaries, but has not found it answer. Recruiters like to get advances and are generally in debt. They all lead depraved lives, so he says, and are given to gambling, women, and drinking.

Has had three of his recruiter's licenses cancelled in the year, because they took coolies to the Demerara depot instead of to him. Rahmat however said that this was false, and that Jehangir had acted purely on suspicion.

At registers again. A defect in the present form is the absence of any column in which to enter the children. Many districts enter them in the column of remarks.

14th – Fatehpur. Called on Collector, but, as he had only just joined, he could give no information. Interviewed the *tahsildar*, who said there was a case against a recruiter with reference to a woman some six months ago. It was not established. From a respectable Musalman whom I met promiscuously I heard of a case in which a woman having deserted her husband lived with a recruiter for some time until the latter tried to get her registered, on which she left him and rejoined her husband, while one of the recruiters (the wrong one by his account) got imprisoned over the business. Recruiters publish generally their readiness to pay Re. 1 for each man brought and Rs. 2 for each woman. Even *patwaris* and *chaukidars* occasionally do a little business in this way.

Abdul Rahim, recruiter, came to see me. Was formerly a *muharrir* in the Kirwi settlement. Says that Fasad Ali, a resident of Gorakhpur, entertained the recruiters about whom there was trouble.

They have left.

Has worked himself under Mazhar Husain of Cawnpore at Rs. 7 a month; has never, so he says, held a sub-contract. Work is now closed for the season. Visits villages and is never interfered with, but the district is not a good one.

Denies that *patwaris* or *chaukidars* ever bring recruits. There is another recruiter who is away now at Cawnpore, and who is going to work for French Colonies as well as for Demerara and he (informant) intends to do the same. Cannot give the name or residence of a single returned coolie. Police do not interfere. No *bandish*.

The usual remark he hears in the villages is – 'Why should we go so long as one can earn a quarter *anna* here to a place from whence there is no knowing whether we shall ever be allowed to return?'

Rae Bareli a good recruiting-ground and Partabgarh a bad one; because although adjacent, and Partabgarh the most populous, the landlords of the latter district take more pains to find their people work than do the Rae Bareli landlords. This, he says, is *mashur*. Complains of having to apply for his certificate on an eight-*anna* stamp. Also of people telling the coolies that the recruiter speaks falsely.

Examined registers.

Clerk has never received a fee.

Register is on a printed form. Duly signed and certificate printed. Register 'number' by batch, and not for any period. No entries since November, 1861. A very large number of people from Partabgarh registered here in former years.

Recruiter says that in this district *chaukidars* are enjoined to keep a sharp lookout for *Arkatis*, and consequently that there are none. Always in the district wears his *chapras*, to show that he is not an *Arkati*.

Banda a good district for recruits, because the people are both strong and *gharib*.

Examined misls of cases. In the case of Musammat Nasiban and child, the woman declared that the recruiter had kept her for six months, and had got her sent to Calcutta against her will after promising to get her sent back. She told the Protector that she had never been before the Magistrate.

Another coolie in the same batch told the Protector that he could not speak to the Magistrate. Both of these stories were disproved on examination before the Magistrate of Fatehpur.

I omitted to note that, on the 12th, Jehangir Khan reported to me that on the 11th, after I had visited his depot, a policeman came and ordered a coolie to be released. Could give no reason for this, and insinuated that it was purely unwarrantable interference. I said nothing, but drove down in the evening and took the depot by surprise. The *chaprasi* then said that the *Brahman*, whom I had noticed at my first visit as looking nervous, had gone out to the *thana*, and brought in a *sepoy* to insist on his being allowed to take away his things; that Jehangir Khan has asked for payment for the number of days for which the man had had food. The *sepoy* made the *Brahman* pay and off he went. It also transpired that the man had a case about land before the High Court, and had shown his paper about it to induce the *sepoy* to interfere. Two things seemed demonstrated: one was that Jehangir had imputed motives to the police for which he had really no grounds, and the other was that this *Brahman* was deliberately, apparently, attempting to procure free lodging. Having a case, he never could have seriously intended to enlist for any sort of service; but, on seeing me, grew fearful that there would, after my going, be no retreat, unless he made off at once.

I find that it is not at all an uncommon thing for coolies to have money about them, sometimes as much as 8 or 10 *rupees*. The recruiters take charge of these sums for them and return the money in Calcutta but there are several disadvantages in the plan. The recruiter, for instance, having got the money under pretence of keeping it safe, can keep the coolie in subjection if he shows any sign of changing his mind by threatening to retain the money altogether. On the other hand, I found cases when at registration the coolie has mentioned (just to make sure) that he has money in deposit, and the Magistrate has at once suspected the recruiter of foul play, and not unnaturally so. Therefore I think that the recruiters shall be absolutely forbidden to receive any money in deposit, or property of any sort.

April 18th, Lucknow – Ewaz Ali (Trinidad Sub-Agent) and Mr Ezra (a Jew), Sub-Agent of French Colonies, came to see me.

Complaints made about Mainpuri. Until the other day all had gone well, but with a change of Collectors all had gone wrong, and women were being rejected wholesale and without reason. This new Collector is the same officer whose trial of some recruiters at Allahabad in 1876 created such a long correspondence. From Mr Ezra I found that the Passover lasted from 4th April to 11th April.

Also that Rupa, returned emigrant from Guadeloupe, re-emigrated to that colony last November with his wife and two children.

Rupa gave as a reason for few people returning from Guadeloupe, that drinking and gambling were very prevalent there, and that the bounties offered tempted people to remain, the said bounties however being quickly gambled away. Land also is freely offered, and there are many coolie *zamindars* who themselves import coolies.

Cawnpore police still complained of. They abstain, as directed by the Magistrate, from cross-questioning the coolies, but now keep the people waiting at the *thana* and use abusive language. Mr Ezra admitted that after several cases had occurred in which the Agra police had brought charges against his recruiters, he asked that the system of taking coolies to the *thana*, for registration might be introduced, but that he had repented of it ever since, and that his recruiting operations were seriously interfered with by police oppression.

Ewaz Ali admitted that the system of receiving the property of coolies in deposit existed, and says he keeps a register; coolies would otherwise steal from each other, and there would be frequent police cases in the depots, which would hinder work. This may well be the case, but the practice of receiving deposits must come under regulation. There was a case last year in which a coolie's deposit of Rs. 250 formed the subject of a long enquiry, and it turned out that the man had misappropriated the money from his master.

On one occasion lately a Panjabi with his wife and children went off to Calcutta as coolies with Rs. 200 in their possession, which the man had made during the Cabul war as a *jamadar* in the Commissariat. They were bound for Fiji, and were going to invest their money in such articles of luxury as they had heard from an old coolie were in demand amongst the Colonial Indians, such as *tika* marks for women, *surma*, scents, &c. That, no doubt, was case where they thought Fiji with its population of 7 or 800 Indians as good a market as Demerara with 80,000 Indians.

A notable case of coolie success was mentioned in Kedarnath, a resident of Lucknow, who went off 12 or 15 years ago. Somehow or other he has got an appointment as native doctor of coolie ships, and was met 4 years ago at Benares on his way to Jaunpur to invest Rs. 1,000 in the *attar* for which Jaunpur is renowned, to sell again in Demerara. This man has carried off from Lucknow every relative he could induce to go with him.

About 20 old Jamaica coolies have enlisted this year for Fiji.

The sub-agents complain that the Deputy Collector at Shahjahanpur allows his *amlah* to use language towards the coolies calculated to frighten them. Also that the Deputy *Saheb* at Moradabad refuses to register women. Mr Ezra asked me to look up while in Agra the cases in which his recruiters were prosecuted.

19th April – Examining Lucknow registers all day; comparing entries taken from register in other stations.

Khan Muhammad, Panjabi, a returned emigrant from Demerara, came to see me. His story, as proved by the papers he produced, was rather singular. Having served as a police cavalry *sowar* through the mutiny, he took a good conduct discharge in 1861. Remained in Lucknow for one year or so and then, having quarreled with his wife and her relatives, started for Demerara, leaving the wife and son behind.

Remained in Demerara some 18 years; made a large amount of money. Married again and returned with his second wife and family last year.

Left land and money in Demerara with a son-in-law, and brought back a large sum of money as well. Having purchased '10 ploughs of land' in his native village in the Gujranwala district and settled the second wife there, he was now travelling about in search of his first family. Was in high spirits at having heard that his son had been seen as a bandsman in a native infantry Regiment at Bareilly in 1878, and came to see me before going to Bareilly, as he thought he would like to get a sub-agency, and felt sure that he could recruit more successfully than any one who had not been abroad. I talked with him for a long time, and found him in his common sense and independent way of thinking far more European than native. He had a large silver medal presented to him by his employers and engraved with a flattering testimonial, of which he was very proud.

The following was one of many testimonials:

> Khan Muhammad has been in this estate for the past 12 years, for two of which he was building watchman. The other 10 years he has been head coolie driver, and as such was a most valuable man, owing to his great tact with his countrymen, being firm with but still very kind to them. He is intelligent, honest, and sober, and to any one requiring a superintendent he is worthy of a trial. He has also been a rural constable for 12 years.
>
> (Sd.) THOMAS LAW
> Plantation Aurora, Essequibo.

In Khan Muhammad's opinion, now that drinking has been stopped, coolies will remit more money and return in greater numbers than heretofore. Much money used formerly to be squandered in drink. Planters used to allow coolies rum from the plantation 'still.' This is now strictly forbidden under heavy penalties, and rum can only be bought under license, and restrictions even when required, as it is sometimes for men who are working in water repairing embankments.

Believes that if every coolie were forced to return when his 10 years expired, and was offered a bounty for each man he could bring with him on re-emigrating, that emigration would receive a great impetus.

Was very happy in Demerara. Finds in Hindustan so much dishonesty. Has already had his house broken into by thieves.

Returned in 1880. When he left there were three brothers, *Brahmans* and belonging to the Gonda district, who had in three years each put by the sum entitling them to have their indentures cancelled. They had lodged the sum for their passages and Rs. 1,400 besides, and were to follow in the next ship. They were splendid workmen, he said.

Postage on letters is handed in in cash, and the Negro postmen pocket the cash and tear up the letters, or used to do so, and are much distrusted.

A coolie under him had been in Surinam and Trinidad. According to his account the Surinam coolies could not earn so much as those in Demerara, nor were they so well housed or looked after: hence there is greater sickness amongst them. But the Dutch are kind masters, whereas the French masters have, amongst Demerara coolies, got the reputation of being unkind and of beating their coolies. Mauritius on the other hand, is in good repute with those who are not fond of hard work, on account of the system of monthly wages, and not task-work, being in force.

But in Khan Muhammad's opinion, for hardworking men the task system is the best, and under it much money may be earned. The coolies resort much to the Banks to deposit their savings.

Brahmans are much given to setting up as *Padris*, otherwise they work like other castes, since there is no work, like ploughing, which is forbidden to them by their religion.

Formerly there was much drunkenness and little religion; now there is less drunkenness and much more religion. Religious books both for Hindus and for Musalmans are imported from Calcutta; eight Masjids have been built within his recollection, and many low-caste men have been reclaimed from drunken habits by conversion to Muhammadanism.

Masters are very kind to their men, and at marriages give flour, &c., and animals for slaughter, according to the caste of the coolies.

American flour far superior to that sent from India and much appreciated by coolies. Also American rice and corn-flour; salt-fish from Newfoundland good and plentiful. Fresh fish very plentiful and easily caught. Apparently no fault to be found with anything.

Khan Muhammad had by him a lot of envelopes ready addressed to his former employers, so at his request I wrote a letter to them, telling them what he was doing, and sending messages to such a number of coolie friends that I thought he never would stop.

I also found out from the Army List which regiment it was that his son had been seen with. It proved to be now stationed in Assam, and to be one of the regiments under orders for disbandment. The change from high hope to despair in the man was very touching, but I telegraphed the circumstances to the Commanding Officer of the regiment, and I have since been informed that Khan Muhammad has recovered his long-lost son after all.

After comparing my extracts from the Benares register with the Lucknow register, I found that a large number of men registered at Lucknow on 4th May, 1878, for Natal were again registered at Benares on 8th July, 1878, for Trinidad. Another batch registered at Lucknow on 8th October, 1877, for Trinidad were again registered at Benares on 11th October for Jamaica.

Balua, *Kori*, registered at Benares on 11th October, 1877, for Jamaica, was again registered at Lucknow on the 24th October, 1877 for British Guiana. I only discovered this because I happened to have visited the homes of many of the men in these batches and recognised their names again at Benares.

One or two of them were men to whom I had promised to write, and but for this discovery I should never have found their addresses.

As it was, it took some time to discover the ships in which one or two of them had sailed.

21st April – At Cawnpore replying to letters, writing to Collectors, and reading up papers received

22nd April – Called on the Collector by appointment, as I had had some correspondence about the rule of reporting to the police, which had not effected cancellation. Reasoned out the matter, and Collector agreed to cancel the obnoxious order. Went over the registers and pointed out deviations. Called at the French depot, but found that recruiting could not commence before the 1st May. Muzaffar Ali's recruiters, who were here when I last visited Cawnpore, have removed elsewhere.

23rd April – Left in the afternoon for Etawah.

24th April – At Etawah. The Collector had already explained by letters that only one coolie, so he understood, had been brought for registration, and that being busy with a case, he had told the man to come next day, but had not again seen him. We drove down together to the town depots, two in number.

A fair amount of room and the usual amount of dirt. Rooms enough to admit of women being separated; coolies in both.

A woman from Etawah, and her daughter, who seemed fully to understand where they were going, said in reply to the Collector that she had left a son at home, which sounded bad, until the son's age was given as over twenty. Another woman with three children said she was going because her only relative refused to support her.

Examined registers at *kutchery*. No certificate, and register not signed. Register number on no system; runs on for two years.

Names of those rejected not entered. The only district I have yet seen where any 'occupation' is entered other than 'labour' or 'cultivation.'

In 1879 the registering officer noted against every name the result of his cross-examination of the coolie, a most laborious work when there are many registered.

All children by name entered in column of remarks.

Etawah seems a great *naka* for people from Native States, especially from Gwalior.

Collector agrees in thinking that Civil Surgeons might well register. So, by the way did Dr Walker, Inspector General of Prisons, whom I met on my way from Allahabad.

Read over the correspondence, which took place last November, when the Deputy Collector was charged with having intimidated coolies by telling them that they would be deprived of caste.

In explanation, the Deputy Magistrate, instead of specially denying the expressions imputed, simply said in general terms that the accusations were false, and denied that any coolies had ever been terrified by such statements; which is somewhat different to saying that such statements were never used.

The District Superintendent of Police gave me as his opinion that cases of deception were very rare, and that the coolies well knew what they were about. Did not know where the depots were any more than any other officer I have met, barring the Collector of Azamgarh, who knew about where the depot was.

25th April – At Mainpuri. On arrival five women, about whose rejection some days before I had principally come, were brought up to tell their own story. I carefully questioned them as to their residence, their reasons for being here instead of in their own districts, and their knowledge of what they were undertaking. To all my questions I received satisfactory replies.

1. Was accompanied by a strong boy of 12 or so, her son. Had no relatives left.

2. A young Thakurain of Muttra, who lost her husband here last February, the death was registered at the *thana* (of which the Magistrate had been informed). Has been living on charity ever since.

3. A *Brahman* widow, also from Muttra, has been living for some time on *bazaar* charity.

4. A Musulmani, belonging to some out-district, who had evidently been on the town.

5. A wretched-looking creature, a young widow, half starved, who said she had no relatives and was glad to get work.

Husain Bakhsh, the recruiter here, is on monthly pay, the contract being with one Mahiput Singh, who is now unlicensed, but who was formerly a licensed recruiter.

The registration clerk attended with registers. No fee ever drawn. Matter was referred to the Protector, and from reply it appears that the Government, North-Western Provinces, must sanction as a special case for each district on application.

Register is in due form, but is bound up in brown paper covers. Under the heading 'depot whence to proceed' is given the full address of the Calcutta depot, the first district where I have so far found a similar entry.

Certificate appended in earlier but not in later years.

Magistrate does not sign register, but initials for each coolie passed. Occupation column contains 'labour' or 'cultivation.'

In the Inland Emigration Register I find that the column for occupation is wisely left out.

Column of 'number' in register filled in last year for each batch and this year by the year.

The numbers recruited in this district are annually increasing:

1876	23	1879	62
1877	Nil	1880	113
1878	Nil	1881	181

and for 1882 there have been for three months 133, while 44 more have been registered for inland emigration.

Against a batch of 12 brought up for registration in 1879-80 I find the following remarks:

'2 from Mainpuri, 2 from Etah (husband and wife), registered. The rest do not account why they are here (sic); should be registered in their own register.'

Against another batch; 'Of these 14 recruits 9 belong to other districts; of the 9, 3 are women and 4 boys of 18; of the 5 belonging to Mainpuri 2 refuse to go. A man (Dilawar) remains and 2 women; but as to the two remaining women enquiry will be made through the police, as the recruiter's proceedings seem suspicious.'

'Behari complains that he has paid Rs. 2 to the recruiter and was promised service at Cawnpore. Pending this enquiry I suspend the recruiter's license.'

Now in this self-same register against the name of the man Behari is written the word 'absent,' and of any further enquiry I could get no evidence. It is impossible not to read in the whole of the above note a cruel animus. Out of the 9 thus rejected summarily for belonging to 'other districts,' one belonged to the Native State of Dholepur, where of course there would be no registration.

I now come to the last batch put up for registration. It seems that the batch before had been to the Deputy Magistrate, and that a woman in it (the clerk was my informant), a prostitute, who had only lately come out of jail after being imprisoned for theft for 3 months, refused at time of registration to proceed.

The Collector then ordered the next batch to be brought to him. On the 14th April 8 were produced, of whom 5 were women belonging, as I have already noted, to other districts. They were all rejected and bracketed with the following remark.

'Not satisfied that they have not come by recruiter's inducement; no relative present.'

I had called on the Collector early, but failed to see him. So he came to see me while I was busy with the registers. With reference to his remark I understood him to say that he held that in every case when a woman was described as a widow, a burden of proof lay on both recruiter and recruit to prove that the latter was a widow, and that unless evidence was forthcoming to prove widowhood he should always refuse registration. No reasoning of mine as to the ludicrous travesty of justice involved in expecting a woman who had tramped the country for months hundreds of miles from her home to produce 'evidence' could shake the Officiating Collector's opinion and determination to carry out this procedure: so we parted and I reported the matter to Government.

Later on, Mahiput Singh, the sub-agent, and Hussein Bux, the recruiter, came again.

Coolies are taken from here by camel *dak* to the Etawah station. Mahiput's contract is Rs. 8 for each man and Rs. 9 for each woman loaded at Etawah. Two *annas* a head has to be paid to *Babus* in the *bazaar* for writing out statements which under the law the Magistrate is bound to furnish.

Hussein Bux says that Delhi is a good district for male recruits, but not for female recruits; while Mainpuri, for some reason or other which he cannot explain, is particularly good for female recruits. Query, has it anything to do with the existence of canals, and the (as frequently asserted) impotence of men in canal districts?

Thinks that women recruiters might do well, only that they would get frightened, occasionally at the *sahebs* in *kutcherry.*

The only places in his experience where the police interfere are Agra, Cawnpore and Lucknow.

As there is only one license-holder, his whole time is taken up with recruiting in the *bazaars,* and he has not time to go out to the villages.

Neither sub-agent nor recruiter can name a single returned emigrant.

In the evening visited the depot. A fair amount of room for a small number but rather a ramshackle place. Plenty of houses in the town more eligible. Besides the five women rejected there were several other women in the depot. In fact they were all women. Two or three had been ill for some days with fever. Driving through the town, the number of women about as, compared to men seemed very noticeable.

April 26th – At Agra. When passing through Shikohabad on my way here I found out that there was a recruiter there who, because the town is in the Mainpuri district, is obliged to march his coolies to Mainpuri to be registered; and move them from Mainpuri to Etawah by camel *dak* instead of taking them straight to Etawah by rail.

I should have visited Etah and Farukhabad, but was assured by every one of the sub-agents that registration went on smoothly at those stations.

Examined Agra registers. Slight error in arrangement of columns. Register number runs for the financial year. No certificate. None of those coolies entered who have been rejected. Register written on flimsy paper quite unfitted for a permanent record.

Numbers registered.

1875	110
1876	54
1879	452

1880   1,070
1881   1,843

while for the first quarter of 1882 there are only 120.

April 27th – Inspected depots this morning in company with the Assistant Magistrate. There were two open, one for Natal and one for Fiji; both small and unsuitable. The *Kotwal*, Bundeh Husain, against whom the complaints are made, was away on leave, but the man who was officiating was present, and before him and the Assistant Magistrate direct accusations of oppression were made. The Fiji depot was crammed with coolies, *Thakurs* and Punjabis of a good class. Both the Assistant Magistrate and myself conversed with them, and found them well acquainted with the business in hand.

To *kutcherry*, where I examined the whole of the proceedings in cases instituted against five men (recruiters and *chaprasis*) by the police in October last. These men were convicted mainly on the evidence of police *sepoys* and sweepers for unlawful restraint, and fines were imposed amounting to Rs. 190.

In another case against the same sub-agent in August a constable was the leading witness, that he heard men in the depot crying out that they would not go, yet it was shown that these same recruits had already been registered; and the recruiter's defence was that this very policeman came and told the recruits that if they went they would get no food.

The worst case of all, however, in which I consider most cruel injustice was done, was the case of one Sahibdin, a recruiter for the Demerara Agency.

From such evidence as was recorded it appeared that a woman was recruited who, after a few days, wished to leave the depot. The recruiter refused to allow her to do so until she paid for the cost of the food supplied – a claim which, provided that he had exercised no fraud, he could have established in a civil court, and on which, had it been put in the shape of a claim for board and lodging, he could without resorting to the court have legally detained her property until his claim was satisfied. Apart from that was the absolute certainty that he must take the woman before the Magistrate to be registered, where she could tell her own tale and be allowed to go home. A petition-writer however, living next door, saying that he heard the woman complaining, called in the police, who ran the recruiter in under section 343, Indian Penal Code, for illegal restraint for a period exceeding three days. Before a Native Magistrate he was convicted and sentenced to six months' rigorous imprisonment without the option of fine.

Although to prove illegal restraint for a period exceeding 24 hours it must be proved that the restraint was continuous, it will scarcely be credited that the woman alleged to have been so restrained was never examined as a witness in the case. The evidence was what I call purely hearsay, viz., that of policemen, petition-writers, &c., as to what they had heard the woman say.

My humble opinion of such matters is that where a special law is provided like Act VII of 1871, it should first be ascertained and recorded whether any offence punishable under such law has been committed. Had the recruiter been convicted of using violence, intimidation, or fraud in enlisting the woman, he would still have been liable to fine only, or in default simple imprisonment, but for demanding a claim possibly due, and on what I call inadmissible evidence, the man was punished in this cruel way. His appeal was dismissed because his pleader happened not to be present. I have had a somewhat lengthy correspondence since on this case with the present Magistrate of Agra, who, while admitting that the character of the witnesses was certainly suspicious and peculiar, yet holds that as the woman was at once allowed to depart and could not be found, secondary evidence was admissible. But some people will agree with me in thinking that the fault of the police in allowing the woman to disappear before her evidence could be recorded should have been allowed to weigh in favour of discharging the accused; and further, that until evidence had been recorded in the proceedings to show why the woman's evidence was not obtainable, secondary evidence was not admissible. I could find no attempt in the record to prove that primary evidence was not procurable.

And here I may note that as every one of magisterial experience knows the Indian Penal Code is so elastic that unless the definition given of 'offence' is constantly kept in view, hardly any one goes through life without becoming liable to punishment under it. Where is the use of framing special enactments if they are invariably to be set aside for the Penal Code? In all the cases against recruiters referred to in the Government of India Proceedings, it may be seen that the Penal Code is invariably the law under which recruiters are charged, and how this escaped the notice of the Judges through whom the famous Allahabad case ran the gauntlet, I cannot conceive.

Mr Ezra, Sub-Agent of the French Colonies, came to see me.

Pays Rs. 8 to recruiters of each coolie.

Has the usual complaint to make about the police and about overcrowding on the railway. Is very anxious for permission to recruit in the Native States, where the poverty of the people is said to be very great.

Discussed emigration with the Commissioner, who, on learning the state of affairs at Mainpuri, at once wrote to the Collector; and I have since learnt that the latter at once deferred to the Commissioner's opinion. In fact, later on I found the women of whom registration had originally been refused in the Lucknow depot on their way to Calcutta. At Mainpuri I had noticed that one of them wore some very curious metal ornaments, but that she had not got them at Lucknow; on enquiry about them she produced them all safe from her bundle and was evidently much amused at my remembering the fact. It was satisfactory to see that her property had been respected.

27th – Called on the Collector, who happened to be ill in bed, but at once saw me and forthwith passed an order cancelling the order requiring recruiters to report at the police *thanas,* and passing at the same time another order directing the police to abstain from interference.

It would be difficult to illustrate more forcibly than my experience has done how differently the Magistrates of adjoining districts may act in a simple matter of law and common sense, and it seems to me clearly demonstrated how necessary at every turn it is by clear rules and forcible expression of the wishes of Government to guard against caprice.

28th – At Muttra; examined registers. There has (as at Agra) been a very great falling off in recruits this year as compared to the first quarter of last year.

From November, 1880 to April, 1881 some 464 recruits were registered, while for the period from November, 1881 to April, 1882 only 202 were registered. Good crops are perhaps the cause of this, as registration appears to have been going on smoothly; still no doubt the prosecutions at Agra have caused a great scare, and the police are complained of here as well.

Register in paper covers, not always signed by Magistrate. Register number runs with the financial year. Ages of children noted, which is not the case in every district, yet without it I do not understand how the monthly statement in which adults, minors and infants are separately noted can be properly made out.

Two or three recruiters have been prosecuted here, but no convictions obtained.

The registration clerk, who seems to take some interest in the subject, says he has heard of recruiters employing *Arkatis,* but has never seen one.

In looking over the register, I see large numbers from Native States, particularly from Bhartpur, which Raj has, I find, the reputation of being an uncomfortable one for the subject. There are recruits from Kathiawar, Baroda, Rampur, Hazaribagh, Puna, Ratnagiri, Gorakhpur, Hoshungabad, Sambhalpur, Hyderabad, Cabul, and Kashmir. What would these people do if people were only allowed to be registered in their own districts? The number from Foreign States is 363 out of a total of 1,064.

As at Agra, at Basti, and at other places which were much before the public during the scarcity of 1877-78, there was scarcely any registration during that period. I cannot help thinking that the sub-agents considered grain too dear to make their contract profitable.

A number of recruiters and contractors came to see me during the afternoon. Ram Charan, *Bania,* contracts for 13 rupees 'per pair' to the Muttra station and pays his recruiter 10 *rupees* a month. The latter says he was formerly a *zamindar* of Fyzabad and a neighbour of the sub-agent there, so learnt the business and has held a license three years. Certainly looks respectable and quiet. Ram Charan has applied for a license, but can get no reply.

Anseri is another sharp, smart man who can read and write, and who recruits under contract for the French Colonies
Sheik Naimoollah was formerly in the Aligarh police. Can read and write. Is an intelligent man. Has held a license for three years.

Hussein Bux, licensed for Fiji, has held a license for five or six years. Was formerly a *sowar* in the 8th Bengal Cavalry. Works on salary and has a writer who keeps the accounts. Has been there only 15 days. Was at Delhi before for six months, but came here on account of the difficulty in Delhi of finding the due proportion of women. Men are very plentiful there.

Recruiters talk of Muttra as a place where the influence of *mahajans* is predominant, and that they as a class dislike emigration and oppose it. Police also much complained of; are not interfered with in the villages.

Just before Hussein Bux appeared, the Natal recruiter was complaining of another Natal recruiter who gave his recruits to Fiji, but on Hussein Bux appearing he collapsed and quite forgot the name of the man he was referring to.

Here for the first time the recruiters admitted that *Arkatis* were kept who got Rs. 5 a month, though each says that he does not do it, but that he knows recruiters who do.

Hussein Bux and another strongly disapprove of the idea of women recruiters, while Ram Charan and his merry men strongly approve, but only if returned female emigrants can be found to undertake the work.

No returned emigrants known about here. One man has been heard of as sending money to his relatives.

Another unlicensed contractor, Kwajah Muhammad. He has contracted, so he says, for 20 years. Held a license for 10 years and cannot say why it was cancelled or withheld. This occurred three years ago. Has a recruiter under him.

Auseri says he has worked for nine or ten years without incurring blame.

Another man who came was Nizam Ali, not a prepossessing individual. Looks after a depot for Mir Abbas, a sub-agent who lives at Lucknow. Once held a license and lost it in the post. The contractor is Sayyid Ali (unlicensed) and the licensed recruiter is Rajab Ali, who has gone to Lucknow for more money.

In the evening rode to the city and first inspected Ewaz Ali's depot (Hussein Bux in charge). Well placed, occupying several houses forming part of the inner square of an extensive *Bara,* plenty of room and air; women and men separate. Questioned the women and found them all apparently intelligent as to the reason for their being there; was struck with the noticeable intelligence of one as rather singular. Tried to reach some of the other depots, but it was too late.

29th April – Visited the French depot; rather small and in the centre of the city, but on high ground. Separate rooms, in one of which was a married couple who had not got up when I arrived, and who had an entirely separate room to the rest.

There were two remarkably fine powerful men, a *Thakur* and a *Jat*, from native States.

When I asked the *Thakur* if he knew how long he was going for, he replied in a very frank manner 'Yes, for five years; but if I am treated properly and like the place I shall remain for ten years,' and added that he should like to be able to send money to his home, if there was any chance of his being able to do so.

On to Muzaffar Ali's depot. A large native house in the centre of one of the main streets 3 or 4 stories high, with many rooms, but dirty and evil-smelling to the last degree. A batch of coolies had just gone off, so there was none present.

On to Mir Abas' depot (Nizam Ali in charge). It was rather ludicrous, as I visited each depot I was told what a set of rascals the recruiters were of some other depot; for instance, I was told at Muzaffar Ali's that the woman in Ewaz Ali's depot who seemed so intelligent was not a coolie at all, but an *Arkati*. All, however, joined in saying that Nizam Ali's depot was a disgrace to emigration; that there were a lot of women kept there under promise of marriage, and that no licensed recruiter had been seen there for six weeks.

I found the house full of small rooms, dirty, and generally unfit. Only three coolies were produced, two men and one woman; while there were several Musalmans of rakish aspect in the place, who said they were connections of Sayyid Ali, the contractor, and that both Sayyid Ali and Rajab Ali, the recruiter, had gone to Lucknow for money eight or ten days ago.

A *Bania* came forward and said he was owed Rs. 50 for food supplied, and that he did [not] know Rajab Ali but only Sayyad Ali and Nizam Ali. I then left, and after going some distance one of the opposition recruiters came up and assured me that there were a lot of women concealed in a room who had not been produced.

Going back quickly, I took the people by surprise and found about half a dozen more women who rushed into an inner room, and were said to be *purdah*. Of course I could not on this insist on their coming out, but I made the *Bania* interrogate them at the door of the room. They say that they were not coolies, but were kept by various men[11] living in the house, and Nizam Ali admitted that one of them had a child with her which was suffering from smallpox. Kwajah Ahmad and Hussein Bux came in the afternoon. Cheapness of grain and general well-being of the people leads, they say, to variations in recruiting. Muttra full of women, who beg their way here on pilgrimage to Bindraban and frequent the numerous *Sadha bharat*.

The city people in Delhi are well off, but crowds of men flock there for work from out-districts, and recruiting is brisk.

In the evening came Ram Charan, from whose recruiters I found that the reason for the animus which Hussein Bux had shown in the morning was due to the fact that Sayyid Ali had during Hussein Bux's absence at Delhi seduced away a woman whom Hussein Bux had been keeping. The woman, however, had since left Sayyid Ali, who was now probably in search of her.

Shortly after Rajab Ali appeared as returned from Lucknow. Had not got more than Rs. 25 or so, the rest was to follow. Protested that he had not been away more than 8 or 10 days, but could not explain how his depot was to be maintained, as he had not registered any coolies for six weeks. I think that the other recruiters are probably right in asserting that Nizam Ali and the lot of men I saw all recruit illegally nominally for Natal, but that having failed to get money from Mir Abbas, have given over their coolies to the Fiji Depot. It is said that 11 coolies were thus given over lately. 1 brought all this to the notice of the Collector, who promised to communicate with the District Superintendent of Police and to keep a watch over the proceedings of these people, and agreed with me that no recruiter should be allowed to leave the district without leave from the Collector. If the state of things in this depot in the middle of the city is as the other recruiters assert, then it is evident that either the police do not interfere or are bribed not to.

30th April – At Aligarh, spent the day with the Collector and interviewed Waris Ali, recruiter, an old and respectable man. He has worked for 10 years at Bara Banki, Cawnpore, Bareilly, Aligarh, &c.; says that he gets a fair number here. Bareilly a great place for recruits.

Bara Banki used to be a good place, but has fallen off of late years. Can't say why (query, on account of the railway diverting the road traffic?)

Says that the Deputy *Sahib* who has lately come to Aligarh uses the word *kalapani,* and tries to induce men who have families not to go.

Refers all women brought up alone for police enquiry. Admits, however, that of the last batch of 18, not one was frightened by any language used. Gets men occasionally at Hathras.

The Collector promised to make enquiries and to remove all reasonable ground of complaint. The district people here are, he says, very well off, and very much advanced in intelligence over most other districts, owing to the great spread of education.

1st May – Moradabad. Visited depot. A good native house in the main street, but no coolies in it at present. The sub-contractor here is a *chaudhri* of the butcher caste, an intelligent well-to-do man apparently, though Ewaz Ali afterwards told me that the man was in debt. Has asked for a license, but so far no reply. Keeps a licensed recruiter, Asghar Khan, on Rs. 6. Receives just the same for a woman as for a man, viz., Rs. 10 each.

Examined registers, which I find have been in charge of the Deputy Collector for some time, but the latter not having charge of a sub-division is not legally qualified. This is a point which only struck me later on, and I fear that there has been a vast amount of registration of late years by officers not really qualified under the definition of 'Magistrate.'

Register much too small for writing names and description properly. No certificate. Residents of all districts accepted, but the Deputy Collector admits that he orders a police enquiry in the case of nearly every woman, even when accompanied by her husband, for fear that in the latter case she may have run away from some one else.

There was only one case in which a recruiter had been charged. The record showed that before the Deputy Collector some men from the native State of Rampur said they had been enlisted by fraud, being told that they were to serve as *sepoys*. The prosecution of the recruiter under section 373, Indian Penal Code, instead of under Act XII. of 1871, was ordered, but before the Joint Magistrate the whole case broke down, and the Magistrate in dismissing the charge gave it as his opinion that these men had entered the depot deliberately to obtain free food and had invented falsehoods when it suited them to proceed no further. In the afternoon talked to the contractor and recruiter, who admitted that about ten days ago a *Babu* came with a Mauritius recruiter and a note from the sub-agent (Ewaz Ali) at Lucknow, to say that any coolies collected for Fiji might be given over to Mauritius. There were six recruits in depot who said they were willing and were transferred. The recruiter presented his license for countersignature, then presented the coolies, and registered them for Mauritius and went off, the *Babu* settling the contractor's little bill.

Another point on which I had to set the registering officer right was where he imagined that every coolie *must by law* be first medically examined.

Contractor and recruiter had previously worked for Jamaica and for Demerara. Cannot give the address or name of a single returned emigrant. Seems to them, as to others, quite a new idea to employ returned emigrants as *chaprasis*. One emigrant returned two years ago, bringing Rs. 6,000, but have lost sight of him.

Moradabad is a good place for recruiting on account of the large cities round about both in the Moradabad and in the Bijnor district; keep a small depot at Chandausi.

2nd May – At Shahjahanpur. Examined registers with the Collector. It is quite clear that Ali Jan has gone on refusing to register recruits residents of other districts, though his error was pointed out by the Government of India in 1870. He seems also to have rejected women as being under age to a far greater extent than has been done in any other district. Women who have passed the doctor as aged 25 and even 30 are scored out, the age altered to 16 or 17, and the remark affixed – 'Cannot go, a minor.'

Register number runs by batches. All entered whether passed or not. No signature, no certificate. Initials affixed to each one passed.

Bakar Khan, the recruiter, has held a license for three years. Was before that in the 8th Native Infantry, a smart intelligent man. Gets Rs. 4 a woman and Re. 1 per man produced; all other expenses paid by the *Munshi*. Goes about in the villages, and says that the district is a good one for recruits.

3rd May – At Lucknow. Interviewed Hydar Hussein, who, though frequently in trouble formerly, seems to be still employed. Says that Muzaffar Ali sends his coolies from Fyzabad to Mukamah by boat and saves Rs. 3 a head thereby as against the railway. Suggests that to give each coolie a blanket bought new up-country, to be taken with him on boardship, would be a saving in point of fact, as blankets are so much cheaper up-country, while the coolie would be saved much present suffering from cold. The Trinidad Agency keep blankets in some of their depots, but not so the Demerara. For Fiji and Natal recruiting takes place in the hot weather, when blankets are not required.

Expenses are increased by raising the commission for women and extending depots further up the country, whereas a *dhoti* to each woman on enlistment (cost Re. 1) would cover a vast amount of nakedness, and popularize recruiting very largely.

Opposition to the blankets being given would be offered by those only who contract for the supply in Calcutta.

6th May – At Bahraich. Found one licensed recruiter for Fiji at work, and two others for Trinidad waiting for the season to open work. No sort of difficulty here beyond a want of recruits. All three recruiters of from 12 to 16 years' service, and apparently decent, respectable men. Depot an ordinary native house.

Examined the registers. No certificate; register sometimes signed and sometimes not. Clerk gets two *annas* per coolie. Register number by batches. All coolies entered, but colonies kept separate as at Basti.

9th May – At Bara Banki. No recruits here since 7th February, 1882, and no recruiter at present in the station. There used to be one at Hydargarh in February. The register is printed in sketch-book form. Number runs for financial year. No certificate. Columns of 'address' too narrow. This was formerly a good station.

	Registered		Registered
1874	443	1878	111
1875	185	1879	91
1876	203	1880	59
1877	338	1881	49

In former years men from all parts appear in the register: from Nepal, Cabul, and Gujrat. Can discover no particular reason for the falling off, unless it is that the railway has diverted the road traffic, but then the railroad was running before 1874. I cannot but attribute it in part to the registering officer, whose remarks in the Lucknow register about women I find reproduced here where women are rejected wholesale 'for enquiry,' but as no further entry appears it does not seem as if enquiry were made. In one case a woman was rejected 'pending enquiry from the Collector of her district.' As her district was the native State of Jaipur, it is difficult to see the value of such intelligence.

At Lucknow, writing report, &c.

13th May – Visited Fiji depot this morning. Over 50 coolies, and amongst them the women from Mainpuri. Talked to the people for some time. Out of a batch from Muttra two or three men came forward and complained of not getting *ghi,* though it was given at Muttra, while two women with children at breast asked for an allowance of milk, which also had been given at Muttra. To both these requests the sub-agent promised compliance.

Ewaz Ali and Mir Abbas frequently came to see me.

17th May – Visited depots. In the Fiji depot were 15 or 16 Khyberies, most of them speaking Pushtu only. They were under the leadership of one who had been a *sepoy* in the 26th Native Infantry, a fine-looking man, who said that the lot were all connections of his, and that they fully understood that they were going as cultivators.

In the Ganeshganj depot were a number of fine athletic young men whom I surprised when going through gymnastic exercises (or *kasrat*); they seemed highly amused at being discovered.

A married couple here who had resided in a *taluqdari* village in Rae Bareli had been reported by a servant of the *talukdar* to the police as being unwilling to go. I questioned them about it, and ascertained that the report was quite false, and that, on the contrary, they had fully made up their minds to emigrate.

19th May – Visited the Fiji depot this morning, having heard that a *challan* had arrived from Amritsar. Was quite surprised to see such a fine intelligent lot of men. A large number of them had been in the land transport through the Cabul war, or as they called it 'Lamport,' three of them had been *sepoys* in various regiments. One had been to Malta and others to Abyssinia and ridiculed the idea of being alarmed by a sea voyage. Only one had brought his wife. Most of the others had left families at home and anxiously enquired if they could remit money safely. One man had on patent-leather boots and a silk *dhoti* and another had silver buttons to his jacket.

There was a fine *challan* of *Thakurs* from Etawah and a seedy lot from Lucknow and Rohilkhand.

The relatives of a man who had been enlisted at Sitapur were outside the depot and said that their brother did not want to go. I had the man called out, and after speaking aside with these relatives, he first told a lie by saying that he had never been registered though he had his certificate with him, and then said that he did not wish to go. I asked what he had cost the sub-agent. The account, including registration fees, came to Rs. 3-4, which the relatives at once paid up and took the man off with them. From what took place I gathered that he had left home after a quarrel, and that the relatives had come to make it up.

20th May – On the 20th a number of the Amritsar coolies were taken up under the bye-laws for committing nuisances in a field a long way off from the depot, showing that very little restraint was put on their movements by the sub-agents.

21st May – Ewaz Ali came to me early this morning to say that the parents of a *dhobi* woman, who had enlisted of her own free will, had been registered and was of age, had given a petition to the Magistrate, who had ordered enquiry through the police. That Deputy Inspector Nand Lal, the same who interfered so much last year, had brought down a mob of men to the depot and had made a great disturbance. The woman was with Ewaz Ali, so I cross-questioned her minutely, making Ewaz Ali stand aside. She said that she was a widow; that her parents beat her and would not give her sufficient food; and that she would not return to them, but was determined to emigrate. I said, seeing that she was at least 20 (and had been passed medically as such) that it was entirely optional with her to go or to stay.

On the following Thursday the officer in charge of registration came and asked me if I had heard of the case. He said that on the 22nd the woman appeared before him with her relatives. In the petition it was stated that the girl was *under* 14; had gone out to distribute clothes with all her ornaments on; had been decoyed into a house, stripped of her ornaments and ravished, and brought up for registration. On asking the girl, she said it was all quite true, only that she had been ravished *three* times. Further cross-examination convinced the Magistrate that her tale was false, but as she now said that she wished to go back to her parents, he struck her name off the register.

He was very much surprised when he heard what she had said to me.

27th May – Muzaffar Ali, Sub-Agent for Demerara, came to report fresh interference on the part of the Agra police. Six women, who had already been registered at Muttra, arrived at the halting depot at Agra, where they were accosted by some police *sepoys* and told that the recruiter's tales were all false, and that they would never get any wages, &c.; on hearing which three of the women refused to go further.

Further stated that a bribe was paid to the head-constable not to interfere any more.

Said that he would let me know the names of the *sepoys* accused, but I have heard nothing more from him, and the rest of the batch have gone on to Calcutta.

28th May – Ewaz Ali, Sub-Agent for Trinidad, came to report that the Sitapur recruiter, while bringing in some recruits by camel *dak,* was set upon by a lot of villagers, who insisted by force on a man, who had enlisted, returning home; and, further, refused to allow the other recruits to proceed. Had not yet reported to the authorities. Informed him that nothing could be done until a formal complaint was laid before the Magistrate of the district. Ewaz Ali also told me that the *dhobi* woman (see 21st instant) had been imprisoned in the *thana* from Sunday to Monday morning, and had been threatened by the police.

29th May – Rode up to the *thana*. The *thanadar* admitted having kept the girl at the *thana* from Sunday morning to Monday morning, and that her mother was with her all night; had no warrant, but conceived this his duty.

30th May – Found the man at the depot who knew where the *dhobi* woman lived, and was told that since she had been struck off the register she must have run away from home again, as the parents had been to the depot to enquire if she had returned there.

Went to her house; found the parents and other members of the family all busy at work, whilst the woman who went up for registration was lying on a *charpoy* so stupefied with the fumes of either liquor or opium taken overnight that she could scarcely give intelligible answers. She said that a woman employed at the depot and formerly a neighbour of hers had persuaded her to emigrate; could not say why she told me one thing and the registering officer another.

It seems pretty certain that the girl was good for very little, and would at all events have had some chance of reforming in emigration.

Reported the conduct of the police in thus illegally confining the girl. The mother admitted that she and her daughter had been locked up together in the *thana* for some 18 hours.

5th June – Ewaz Ali and Agha Mirza came today. Agha Mirza said that the same person with whom I found fault at Mutra and reported to the Magistrate (Nizam Ali Shukr and another) were on their trial for illegal recruiting, the recruiter, Rajab Ali, being again away when this happened.

Ewaz Ali had to report that a head-constable named Narain Dutt,[12] of the Ganesganj *thana* (when the *dhobi* woman was detained) had been using language to some recruits who were bathing outside the *thana* that they were frightened and went away, refusing to enter the depot again. I recommended the matter being reported, as he said it could be proved by witnesses.

6th June – A letter from the French Sub-Agent at Cawnpore complaining that a new form of opposition had been set up in the townspeople mobbing and beating the recruiters when they appeared in the streets, and that consequently recruiting was quite at a standstill.

Sent for Ewaz Ali and ascertained that he had heard nothing. However, I went over to Cawnpore by the evening train.

7th June – Visited all the depots at Cawnpore and certainly found the recruiters in a general state of alarm. The French depots had been mobbed and apparently two recruiters had been beaten, while on Monday one of the Trinidad Sub-Agency recruiters had been mobbed and beaten. It seems from what a rival recruiter told me that some people who had lost a child five or six years of age had come to the French depot to enquire and had been refused admittance by the sub-agent, whereupon an outcry was raised that children were being stolen for the sake of their 'oil,' said to be much in favour with thieves, and the term 'Momiaie' brought into use as a term of reproach.[13]

The sub-agent, who was evidently much alarmed and grossly exaggerated everything, declared he had at once opened his depot. The child had been found elsewhere, but the excitement had spread.

I called on the Collector, who promised to have a proclamation issued cautioning persons against interfering with the recruiters without just cause. I had intended going on to Agra if the French Sub-Agent had any complaints from there, but he assured me that the Agra Magistrate had, since I visited that city, taken to visiting the depots weekly, with satisfactory results; there being no longer any cause of complaint against the police, so I returned to Lucknow.

8th June – Ewaz Ali came to report that a recruiter, bringing in a woman, had been set upon by a lot of people near the depot, some of the *chaprasis* from which had come out to help; a policeman joined in the row. Narain Dutt, the head-constable previously complained of, had arrested some of the recruiters or *chaprasis,* and had sent them up to the City Magistrate, charged with assaulting a policeman on duty.

10th June – I hear that in the case abovementioned the *chaprasis* were fined small sums.

Returns have been called for at my instance showing the number of cases instituted against recruiters during the past four years for offences committed under cover of their licenses.

In the Bara Banki return appeared a case tried in September, 1880, in which a recruiter had been convicted of theft, and this case which is now before me shows that however bad the recruiters may be, they have to contend against cruel difficulties.

In this case, which was tried by one of our best officers, a coolie enlisted. After three or four days in the depot he seems to have aroused the recruiter's suspicions, as the latter took him to the registration clerk (there not being enough men apparently of a batch for regular registration), and before the clerk the coolie said he was ready to go, but in a few more days he seems to have refused to go, whereupon he was turned out of the depot and three article of clothing (valued by the magistrate at Re. 1-8) were detained until he should pay for his food.

The coolie complained at the *thana* under a name quite different from that under which he had hitherto been passing. He then went to

Lucknow, where he again enlisted, and after feeding free at the depot for some days went up for registration, and then, apparently, tried to get out of going to Calcutta by making a charge against the Bara Banki recruiter of having taken Rs. 5 as well as the clothes. The man was sent to Bara Banki, and the recruiter was tried and convicted of theft of the clothes and sentenced to six months' rigorous imprisonment with a fine of Rs. 5, although the court expressly stated its disbelief in Rs. 5 ever having been taken from the coolie.

In appeal, the sentence was very rightly stigmatised as unnecessarily severe and the conviction of theft quashed, with a remark that the offence, if any, was criminal misappropriation. The fine, however, which had been paid, was not remitted, and the recruiter had been in jail for one month.

My humble opinion is that, on the evidence, there was no 'offence.' The claim of the coolie to his clothes was one in which some civil courts might hold that the recruiter had a lien on the clothes for board and lodging. To constitute criminal misappropriation 'dishonesty' is essential, and the recruiter simply took such a rude method of recovering his losses from a swindler as many a European official does in this country when he suspects a servant of theft, and turns him out, refusing to pay any balance of wages due until the stolen property has been restored.

And in this case the coolie was by his own admission a common swindler, as he stated that he had originally enlisted at Moradabad; had gone to Calcutta; had there been rejected for defective eyesight; and had received a free pass to Benares and Rs. 6. So in enlisting at Bara Banki again, he must have done so with dishonest intent of living there free, and again the same at Lucknow. His story also about a free pass to Benares should have been tested, as the Protector or Agent is bound to give a pass back to the station of registration.

This case, so similar to the Agra one, demonstrates, I maintain, most clearly that recruiters are the victims frequently of a prejudice created by the constant vituperation which has been levelled at them in past years, and stand in need of the pity of Government rather than still more repressive measures. The figures of district convictions, judging from those already received, will clear them from much of the opprobrium under which they now suffer.

17th June – Visited the Trinidad depot this morning and found over 100 coolies assembled, some of whom have been here for two or three weeks waiting, and were getting anxious to know when they were to be sent away. Complaints made by a large number that some of the townspeople had been telling them that they would get no pay at Trinidad. They wanted to know if it was true.

It was evident from the excited state of these people that some one had been up to mischief. Others asked me if I was quite sure that their caste would not be interfered with; several of these men who had spoken about getting no pay then began to ask for more *attah*. They get three-quarters of a seer of *attah* and a quarter of a seer of dhal, but they said that the *bania* gave short weight, and they asked for cash instead, a matter in which I could not interfere. As all the others who were not frightened by the reports which had been spread were quite satisfied with their food, I put the complaint down to sheer discontent. A woman registered at Etawah said she did not know where she was going, but when I ask her what the Magistrate told her she said Trinidad, or Chini Tat. Several enquired whether they should be able to remit money to their families, and were most anxious on the point. It was the wish to begin earning money that made them anxious about not starting.

Mr Bickers, the registering officer here, tells me that the emigrants, when being registered, very frequently ask now about the possibility, or otherwise, of communicating with their friends.

I have had sent to me within the last fortnight from Calcutta the names of five persons residing in Oudh, for whom remittances have been sent from the colonies months ago, and in one case as far back as two years, but whom Deputy Commissioners (through the police, I presume) have been unable to find.

I have, with no more difficulty than was involved in giving intelligible instructions, traced the man required in each case within a few days, and, curious to say, nearly every one of the payees had received letters from his or her colonial relative through the post.

D. G. Pitcher, Major
On special duty

NOTES

1. Clerk gets a fee of one *anna* per coolie.
2. The zamindars have since reported that this woman had carried out her intention of marrying again. Meanwhile I had sent Bhawnia a letter, having found after much trouble, that he actually embarked for Natal.
3. This was written at a time when, according to the Cawnpore authorities, the registering officers at Lucknow were less particular than those at Cawnpore.
4. Probably an *Arkati*.
5. In the Lucknow district.
6. It seems that the coolies could not procure stamps but gave cash with their letters to the postman.
7. *Mirch* (a corruption of Mauritius) is a name very commonly used of emigration colonies.
8. Traced this man to Natal after a long enquiry and wrote to him.
9. She informed me that the police had asked for a subsidy of Rs.10 a month.
10. Another Magistrate took over registration some weeks afterwards, and I soon got a complaint that the case of every single woman was sent to the police for enquiry.
11. Some of these men have, I hear, been since prosecuted for illegal recruiting, and convicted.
12. The District Superintendent of Police transferred this man to another *thana*.
13. *Momiaie* is the name given to persons who are suspected of stealing children and grinding them in oil mills or of hanging them up by their heels when oil is supposed to drop from them. There is apparently a sale for oil so called amongst thieves who think that, rubbed with it, they can elude capture.

GLOSSARY

Abddi	Village habitation site
Ahir	Milk-seller, cultivator
Amlah	Subordinate native officer in an office
Anna	A unit of currency equivalent to 1/16 of a rupee
Arkati	Unlicensed recruiter in northern India
Attah	wheaten flour
Attar	Fragrant oil from rose petals
Babu	Sir, gentleman
Badnam	Not reputable
Bania	Hindu trader or moneylender
Bandish	System of maintaining a guard over the door
Baradari	Summer house with many doors and windows
Barhai	Carpenter
Bazaar	A permanent market
Bedharam	Without any religion
Be din	Without caste or a job
Bhars	Agriculturists
Bhat	Ballad singer
Bhisti	Water carrier
Brahmin	Hindu priest, teacher
Cavalry sowar	Mounted soldier
Challan	A batch of registered recruits
Challandar	Head or leader of a challan
Chamar	Leather worker, labourer
Charpoy	Cot, a common Indian bedstead
Chapras	Badge, a plate worn on a belt as a mark of office
Chaprassi	An official messenger; one hired to accompany recruits to Calcutta
Chattri	A high caste Hindu
Chaudhri	Headman of a craft in a town

Chaukidar	Watchman; a rural policeman
Chittack	Equivalent to about 2 ounces
Chula	Cooking place made of mud, cowdung and unburnt bricks
Dacoit	Thief belonging to an armed gang; a bandit
Daffadar	A person at the head of a body of laborers or soldiers
Dak	Transportation by relays of men and horses/camels
Darwan	Door keeper
Dhai	Place (room) for medical examination of women by nurses or midwives
Dhobi	Washerman
Dhoti	Loincloth worn largely by Hindu men
Diwali	Hindu festival of lights
Ekka	Small one-horse carriage used by Indians
Fakir	Religious ascetic
Gharib	Poor
Ghi	Clarified butter
Guhr	Crop
Gujur	Landholder, agriculturist
Hundis	A form of money transfer; a bill of exchange
Intizam	Administration or arrangement
Jamadar	Leader of individuals in the Indian army
Jat	Largest cultivating caste in northern India
Kabuliyat	A written agreement
Kahar	Bearer, cultivator
Kala pani	literally dark waters
Kancha	Equivalent to about three-quarter of an ounce
Kanungos	Village, district revenue officers
Khafa	Angry
Khidmatgar	Table servant; a person performing some service
Kori	Weaver
Kotwal	Chief police officer in city or town
Kumhar	Potter
Kutcherry	Court house, an office of administration
Lac	A hundred thousand rupees
Lambardar	Headman of a subdivision of a district responsible for revenue collection
Lascar	Sailor

GLOSSARY

Lodh	Cultivator, landholder
Lunia	Field laborer, excavator, saltpertre maker
Mahajan	Merchant, banker
Mashur	Famous, well known, celebrated
Mazduri	Daily hire
Misaj	Short temper, temperament
Muharrir	Lawyer's clerk, writer, scribe
Munadi	Proclamation, public crier
Munsarim	Head Clerk
Munshi	Writer, interpreter, reader, clerk
Naka	Place where pilgrims congregate; point where two roads meet
Padris	Priests, teachers
Pagri	Male headwear, turban
Pakka	Certain, definite
Palki-bearers	Kahars carrying an individual in a palanquin
Pardah	Female seclusion
Pargana	A subdivision of a district
Parwannah	A written order to a subordinate
Pasi	Cultivator, village watchman
Patta	Land lease
Patwa	braid, fringe, tape maker
Patwari	Village accountant, land recorder
Pawn (Paan)	Betel leaf for chewing as a digestive and stimulant
Punchayat	Council of 5 elders of a Hindu village
Reh	Sterile, unproductive soil
Rupee	Indian currency of variable value
Sadha Bharats	Places where food and clothing were distributed to the poor
Saheb	Sir, master, manager, someone in authority
Sarai	Resting place
Sarkar	Refers to government; head of household
Sepoy	Indian soldier in the army of the British East India Company
Seer	Roughly about 2 pounds or 1 liter
Subhadar	Second rank native officer among sepoys
Surma	Powder applied to the eyelids to improve the brightness of the eyes

Tahsil	Administrative unit of a district
Tahsildar	Officer in a tahsil
Talukdar	Landed aristocrat in Oudh
Tapu	Literally an island or colony
Thakur	A person of rank and authority
Thana	Local police station
Thanadar	Officer in charge of a Thana
Tika	A mark made on the forehead
Waris	Husband; without heir or owner
Zamindar	Loosely used term for landholder, large or small
Zenana	A two-wheeled vehicle for the transportation of *pardah* women
Zillah	An administrative district into which British India was divided

FURTHER READING

Books and Journals

Comins, D.W.D. *Note on Emigration from India to British Guiana.* Calcutta: Bengal Secretariat Press, 1893.
Geoghegan, J. *Report on Coolie Emigration from India,* 1874.
Gillion, K.L. *Fiji's Indian Migrants: A History to the End of Indenture in 1920.* Melbourne: Oxford University Press, 1962.
  'The Sources of Indian Emigration to Fiji'. *Population Studies,* 10 (Nov., 1956): 139-157.
Grierson, G.A. *Report on Colonial Emigration from the Bengal Presidency,* 1883.
Mangru, B. *Benevolent Neutrality. Indian Government Policy and Labour Migration to British Guiana, 1854-1884.* London: Hansib, 1987.
  A History of East Indian Resistance on the Guiana Sugar Estates, 1869-1948. New York: Edwin Mellen Press, 1996.
  'Indian Government Policy towards Labour Recruitment for the Sugar Colonies, 1838-1883'. *Journal of Third World Studies,* 1X, 1 (Spring, 1992): 118-138.
Ruhoman, P. *Centenary History of the East Indians in British Guiana, 1838-1938.* Georgetown: The East Indians 150th Anniversary Committee, 1938.
Saha, P. *Emigration of Indian Labour, 1834-1900.* New Delhi: People's Publishing House, 1970.
Sandhu, K.S. *Indians in Malaya. Some Aspects of their Immigration and Settlement 1786-1957.* London: 1969.
Seecharan, C. *'Tiger in the Stars.' The Anatomy of Indian Achievement in British Guiana, 1919-1927.* London: Macmillan Education Ltd., 1997.
Tinker, H.R. *A New System of Slavery. The Export of Indian Labour Overseas, 1830-1920.* London: Oxford University Press, 1974.

Wilson, H.H. *A Glossary of Judicial and Revenue Term and of useful words occurring in official documents*. London: W.H. Allen & Co. 1855.

Yule, H. & Burnell, A.C. *Hobson-Jobson. A Glossary of Colloquial Anglo-Indian Words and Phrases, and of Kindred Terms, Etymological, Historical, Geographical, and Discursive*. Calcutta: Rupa & Co., 1994.

Official Reports

'Report of the Commissioners appointed to enquire into the Treatment of Immigrants in British Guiana', 1870.
'Report by J. Geoghegan on Coolie Emigration from India, 1874.
Annual Reports of the Protector of Emigrants from the Port of Calcutta to British and Foreign Colonies (1871-1885).
'Report on Colonial Emigration from the Bengal Presidency', 1883.
'Note' on Emigration from India to British Guiana, 1893. (D.W.D. Comins).
'Report of the Committee on Emigration from India to the Crown Colonies and Protectorates,' 1910 (Lord Sanderson).

ABOUT THE EDITOR

Basdeo Mangru is a tenured Associate Professor of History at York College, City University of New York. He received his Doctorate at the School of Oriental and African Studies, University of London. He is the author of five books, including *Benevolent Neutrality. Indian Government Policy and Labour Migration to British Guiana, 1854-1884* and *The Elusive El Dorado*, and the editor of three others. Besides, he has published extensively in refereed journals and in anthologies. His research interest is the migration and conditions of Indian labour in the Caribbean, particularly Guyana, in the 19th and 20th century.

INDEX

Abddi, 101-102
Abyssinian War, 65, 183
Act VII of 1871, 16, 50, 74, 80, 172, 180
Act X11 (1871), 180
Afghans, 65
Agra, 45, 123, 160, 175, 187-188
Agra depots
   registers at and conditions in, 170
   colonial sub-depots and police interference at, 171-172
Ajudhia (Fair), 41, 128
Ali, E., 121, 160, 179-180, 184
Aligarh, 117, 129
Aligarh depots, 178-179
Ali, W., 178-179
Allahabad depots
   colonial subdepots and sub-agents at, 148, 153
   location of, 153-154
   recruits at, 153-154
   sub-agent contracts with, and registers at, 153
Allahabad, 28, 35, 45, 82, 143, 146, 148, 153, 155, 156, 166, 173
Amritsar emigrants, 65, 184
Andamans, 115
Arkatis, 14, 16, 29-31, 33, 158, 175-176
Army Act (1881), 43
Assam (tea planters), 13, 68, 155-156
Attah, 189
Attar, 11, 161
Azamgarh depot
   location of, 139
   recruits at, 139-143
   interviews and registers at, 139-141

Badnam, 145
Bahraich depot, 181-182
Bandish, 32, 148, 154, 158

Baka's history, 109-110
Bania, 12, 33, 114, 147
Baradari, 117, 176
Bara Banki depot
   register and annual recruits at, 178-179, 181-182, 187-188
   emigration case at, 179
Basti depot, 71
Bazaar, 36, 43, 71, 111, 167, 169-170
Bazupur enquiries, 108-110
Bedharam, 106
Benares, 45, 67, 72, 112, 117, 143-144, 147, 149, 152, 156, 161, 188
Benares depots
   description and colonial sub-depots at, 146
   recruits and sub-agents at, 146
Bengal Presidency, 13, 20
Benevolent neutrality, 17
Berbice, 111
Beyts, H.N.D., 15
Bhandará system, 29, 77
Bhistis, 155
Bhojpuri, 12-13
Bidesia, 12
Bihar, 12-13
Blankets, 34, 175
Brahman cooks, 29
British Library, 11
British Raj, 11, 20, 122
British West Indian Colonies, 61
Burma(h), 53

Cabul War, 46, 161, 183
Calcutta, 12-15, 19, 29-30, 54, 56, 67-70, 72-73, 80, 82-83, 86, 91, 104, 107, 112, 117-118, 122, 124, 132, 137, 145-146, 148, 181, 188-189
Calcutta Agency (Demerara), 107

199

Calcutta depots, 29, 31, 67
Calcutta Emigration Meeting, 54
(Camel) dak, 27, 169-170, 185
Camp Bukus, 106
Caribbean
    emancipation and immigration into the, 13-16
Cantonment Magistrate, 52
Castes (N.W.P.), 94-99, 128
Caste dinners, 25
Cawnpore, 11-12, 45, 119-121, 165, 186
Cawnpore depots
    personnel, 119
    colonial sub-depots, 119
    recruits, 120-121, 186
    complaints, 119-120, 186
    registration stations at, 119
    physical conditions and location of, 119
Caylor, J., 146-147, 156
Central Provinces, 26
Chalan, 39, 82, 148, 153, 183
Chand Sarai
    register and trade custom at, 113-114
Chaprassis, 29-31, 40, 47, 55, 64, 67, 112, 137-139, 147, 153-155, 159, 171, 180, 187
China, 44, 113
Chit, 70
Cholera, 139, 154
Chota Nagpur, 13
Chulas, 118
Circular No. 88 (1879), 48, 142
Chaukida, 100-107, 110, 112, 116, 157-158
Civil Surgeon, 53, 80, 118, 132, 135, 137, 166
Collector of Jaunpur, 69-70
Colonial Agents, 16, 19, 70
Colonies
    popularity of, 66, 104
Consolidated Ord. 4 of 1864, 15-16
Consular Agent (Karikal), 38
Contract
    between Agent & Sub-Agent, 30, 79-81
    between Sub-Agent & recruiter, 30, 82-83
Cutchery (Kutchery), 47, 52, 71, 123, 134, 141, 147-148, 166

Dacoits, 112
Darwan, 125, 133, 149
Daudnagar registers, 109
Delhi, 122, 125, 155, 169, 178
Demerara (British Guiana), 18-19, 22, 28, 35, 42-43, 56, 60, 66, 73, 86-88, 91-92, 104, 107, 112, 118, 121, 124, 128-129, 140-141, 143-144, 148, 152, 155-156, 163, 171, 181
Depots
    physical improvements in, 32, 36, 117, 146
    registers in, 33
    food served in, 29, 32, 88
    defects in, 32-33
    arrangement and management of, 34, 86-88
    personnel in, 30-31, 130
Diseases, 139
Dhoti, 34, 55, 181

East Indian Railway, 132
Eden, A., 53
Emigrants
    wives of, 27
    commissions for, 35, 79, 82, 120, 155
    medical examination of, 15, 47, 72
    physical conditions of, 34-35, 167
    complaints by, 32
    ages of, 83
    property of, 25, 62, 159
    as entrepreneurs, 11, 161
Emigration
    obstacles to, 44, 59, 65, 148
    inducing, 59-60
    attitude towards, 43-45
    up-country, 58
    impact on villagers, 27, 63, 148
    advantages of, 62
    popularity of, 62, 65-66, 130
    encouragement of, 63-65, 86-87
Emigration Agent (Calcutta, 16-17, 26, 68, 103
Emigration Bill (1880), 18, 59
Emigration Fund, 69
England (London), 44, 92, 151
Emerson (Mr.), 148
Etawah depots, 165-166, 183

INDEX

European Magistrates, 47-48
European planters, 111
Ezra (Mr.), 160, 173

Factory work (British Guiana), 87
Family emigration, 57-59
Famine Commission, 44
Fatehpur depots
   interviews, 157
   recruits, 158
   registers, 158
   cases and complaints at, 159
Fiji, 28, 46, 66-67, 104, 117-118, 120, 154, 156, 171, 175, 180-181, 183
First World War, 14
Flour-eater, 30
French Colonies, 35, 61-62, 66, 123, 160, 173, 175
Fyzabad, 42, 45, 58, 71, 125, 134-135, 152, 175, 181
Fyzabad depots
   registers in, 128
   recruits at, 128-129
   personnel and physical conditions in, 128
   districts and interviews at, 129

Garden Reach, 14
Ghi, 32, 88, 154, 182
Gillander, Arbuthnot & Co., 14
Gonda-Babraich Railway, 46
Gonda depot, 117-118, 134
Gorakhpur depots
   registers, 137
   interviews, 137
   conditions at, 139
Govt. of Bengal, 15, 142
Govt. of India (Indian Govt.), 11, 14, 17-18, 44, 52, 57, 86, 142
Grenada, 117
Grierson, G.A., 18

Hakim-ke-mizaj, 104, 130, 133, 154
Hindustan(i) 60, 86, 111, 122-123, 151, 163
Howrah, 120, 138
Hulas Khera (interviews), 116
Hundis, 58

Imigration Agent-General (British Guiana), 86
indenture system, 14, 60-61
India Office Library, 11, 17
Indian Civil Service, 11
Indian Emigration Bill (1883), 23
Indian slave trade, 16
Inland Emigration Act and Register, 50, 167
Indian women, 20-21, 27, 54-57
Indian Penal Code, 172-173, 180

Jacob (Mr.), 156
Jamadar, 66, 138-139, 149, 161
Jamaica, 112, 122, 164, 180
Jaunpur depot
   recruits in, 143
   numbers registered at, 144
   physical conditions of, 143-144
   women in, 143-145
Jews, 11, 28, 43, 129, 136, 160

Kala pani, 47, 111, 132, 148, 179
Kanungos, 65
Karachi, 65
Khan, J., 153, 157, 159
Kheri district (Oudh), 26
Khidmatgars, 121
Khyberies, 182-183
Kingsley (Canon), 39
Kotwal, 120, 129, 133, 171
Kutna Valley and resettlement, 26, 101

Lal, Jia, 106-107
Lambardars, 63, 106, 110, 112, 116, 124
Land settlement (grants), 61
Laissez faire, 20
Law, T, 162
Lieutenant-Governor (British Guiana), 57
Local depots
   management of, 29-36
   payment to emigrants in, 29-30
Lyall, A., 20-21
Lubbock, N., 17
Lucknow, 18, 27, 41, 52, 71, 73, 102-103, 105-107, 111-114, 116, 118, 152, 183
Lucknow depots
   recruiting stations, 164, 181

colonial sub-depots at, 165, 181
interviews, 161-164
recruits at, 164, 181
complaints and rejections in, 163
registers at, 161, 164, 182
personnel at, and physical
conditions of, 164
Lucknow registers
examination and results of, 51, 103-106

Madras (Chennai), 13
Malta, 65, 183
Mauritius, 15, 35, 58, 66-67, 113, 124, 138, 145, 163, 180
Mainpuri depots
rejections, 166
recruits, 167
annual registration and registers in, 167-168
physical conditions at, 170
colonial sub-depots at, 170
pardah women and interviews at, 168
Mazduri, 107
Medical Inspector (Emigrants), 56, 69
Minimum wages (British Guiana), 87
Mirch (Mirchias), 47, 113, 138, 145
Misr, Ganga Din, 22, 110-111
Momiaie, 78, 186
Moradabad depot
description of, 179-180
registers, 179
prosecutions and contractor at, 179-180
Moses, J., 123, 146, 153
Mufassal (Magistrate), 14-17
Muhammad, Khan, 22, 161-164
Munsarim, 127
Mutiny (1857), 20, 22
Munshi, 120, 127, 133, 181
Muttra depots
registers, 174
recruits, 174-176
recruiters in, 174-176

Nakas, 45, 125, 130-131, 166
Natal, 28, 35, 65-66, 116-117, 121-122, 124, 164, 171, 181
Native contractors, 175
Native States, 11, 45, 174, 176
Nepal (Nepaulese), 41, 129, 137, 145, 182

North-Western Provinces and Oudh (United Provinces), 11, 13-14, 18-21, 29, 39-40, 52-53, 65-66, 103, 119, 127, 132, 142, 145, 152, 167
castes in, 94-99
distribution of emigrants in, 84-85, 89-90

Oil mills, 43, 86
Oudh and Rohilkhand Railway, 46, 55, 132

Palki-bearers, 46,
Pakka, 82
Panchayat, 140
Panjab(is), 43, 171
Pardah (women), 34, 177
Parehtah and Moharia Khurd, 115
Pargana, 50, 52, 70
Parshad, M., 147, 156
Parwannah, 64
Passover, 28, 136, 160
Patna-Babraich Railway, 136
Patwaris, 30, 65, 157-158
Pawn (paan), 32
Peshwar hillmen, 65
Pioneer of India, 16
Ploughmen, 34, 135
Pitcher, D.G., 11, 18-20, 21-23
report of, 18-20, 25-78, 99
Diary of, 22-23, 101-190
recommendations of, 74-78
appointment and instructions to, 18-19
interviews by, 20-21
Population Census of India (1881), 23
Police officers and inquiries, 41, 125, 132, 170
Postal (postage) communication, 60, 123
Protector of Emigrants (Bengal), 25, 37, 50, 80, 103, 188

Queensland, 65, 68

Rae Bareli depot
registration, 126-127
caste groups, 127
complaints at, 126
personnel in, 126
Rajputana, 41

INDEX

Railway Company's servants, 67, 131
Rail transportation, 67-68, 155
Rangoon, 135
Rates of pay, 35, 87
Rations, 73-74, 88
Recruiters
   class, 36
   character, 36-37, 137, 183
   remuneration, 35, 82
   recruiting methods of, 16, 41, 72, 140-141, 144, 172
   attacks on, 36, 43
Recruiting stations, 27-28, 84-85, 89-90, 130-131
Recruiting system
   in Trinidad Agency, 33-36
   in Demerara Agency, 29-32
Registration
   numbers registered and year, 84-85
   fees for, 53, 72
   attention to, 47-48, 50, 52
   reforms in, 46, 52-53, 71-72
Rejects, 48, 153
Remittances, 58-59, 63, 71, 73, 91-92, 161-163
Resident (Hyderabad), 49
Returned emigrants (returnees), 43, 56, 60, 62-63, 66, 70-71, 116, 122, 148-149, 151, 160-163
Resettlement (in India), 78
Return passage, 87
Revenue & Agriculture Office (Calcutta), 26
Rice-eater, 29
Rum-drinking (colonies), 61, 160, 162-163

Sadhabarts (Benares, Muttra), 42, 149
Salisbry (Lord), 17, 20
Sarais, 42, 149
Sarkar, 45
Scarcity (1877-78), 46, 152, 175
Sepoy, 49, 120, 125, 139, 159, 171, 180-181, 183-185
Shahjahanpur registers, 180
Ships
   Hermione, 117
   Sylhet, 117
   Jet, 107
Singh, Chandi, 116
Singh, Prag, 106

Small Cause Court, 18, 118
Sowar(s), 161
St. Helena, 111
Subagents, 16, 42, 67, 92
Suriname, 12, 107, 154-155, 163

Tahsil (Tahsildar), 64, 77, 106, 134, 139, 142, 157
Talukdar (Oudh), 64, 156, 183
Tapu, 66
Thana (Thanadar), 77, 110, 112-113, 140, 160, 173, 185-187,
Thika, 87
Thomson, R., 119
Tika, 11, 161
Tinker, H., 11, 17
Trans-Atlantic passage, 14
Trans-Gogra & trans-Gumpti Districts, 143
Transportation: Improvements in, 67-69, 149
Trinidad, 22, 35, 82-83, 104, 114, 120-121, 127-128, 138, 141, 143, 151, 154-155, 164, 181, 189
Trinidad depot, 29, 32, 72-74
Trollope, A., 39, 61-62
Twenty Four Parganas, 13, 18

Uttar Pradesh, 11-12

Village India, 12, 22
Voyage
   length of, 66, 122
   fear of, 151
   food served on, 122

Wealthy (returned) immigrants, 62-63, 71, 145, 161-163
West Indian Colonies (Islands), 28, 56
West India Committee, 17
Women emigration, 49, 54, 56

Zamindar, 12, 19, 42, 113-114, 124, 134-135, 138, 141, 160, 175
Zenana carriage, 55